The Warrior

Who Would Rule Russia

Benjamin S. Lambeth

Prepared for the United States Air Force

RAND

50ᵗʰ
Project AIR FORCE
1 9 4 6 – 1 9 9 6

RAND is providing analytical support to the Deputy Chief of Staff for Plans and Operations, Headquarters United States Air Force, on a variety of global security trends and their possible impact on USAF institutional needs over the next two decades.

This report was written in connection with that effort. It offers a detailed portrait of retired Russian army Lieutenant General Aleksandr I. Lebed, who rose to prominence three years ago as the commander of Russia's 14th Army in Moldova and has since been appointed security adviser by the recently reelected President Boris Yeltsin. Lebed, who himself finished a surprisingly strong third in the June 16, 1996 presidential election, promptly joined forces with Yeltsin and helped ensure the latter's winning of a second term in the subsequent July 3 runoff. Because of his current role as the new point man in Russian security affairs and his manifest ambition for higher office, he warrants careful attention by American military leaders and defense planners.

A richer understanding of Lebed's declared outlook on a broad range of issues can offer valuable insight into what kind of Russia the United States will have to deal with in the years ahead, for better or for worse. The analysis presented here—drawing on his many statements and interviews over the past two years—looks beyond the often superficial characterizations of Lebed that have until recently been put forward by the media, to develop a fuller picture of what he actually believes and where he stands on fundamental issues. It portrays him as a respected professional of strong authoritarian bent and unsure devotion to the idea of democracy, yet one who has spo ken out strongly against crime and corruption, appears committed to a market economy, and is less aggressively nationalistic than many Western accounts have suggested.

This report was written for the Strategy and Doctrine Program of RAND's Project AIR FORCE. It should be of interest to USAF officers and other members of the U.S. defense establishment concerned with Russian political development, foreign and defense policy, prospects for military reform, and security relations with the United States and its allies.

PROJECT AIR FORCE

Project AIR FORCE, a division of RAND, is the Air Force federally funded research and development center (FFRDC) for studies and analysis. It provides the Air Force with independent analyses of policy alternatives affecting the development, employment, combat readiness, and support of current and future aerospace forces. Research is being performed in three programs: Strategy and Doctrine; Force Modernization and Employment; and Resource Management and System Acquisition.

In 1996, Project AIR FORCE is celebrating 50 years of service to the United States Air Force. Project AIR FORCE began in March 1946 as Project RAND at Douglas Aircraft Company, under contract to the Army Air Forces. Two years later, the project became the foundation of a new, private nonprofit institution to improve public policy through research and analysis for the public welfare and security of the United States—what is known today as RAND.

CONTENTS

Aleksandr I. Lebed remains all but unknown to most Americans. Yet in the wake of Russia's presidential election on June 16, 1996, which pitted Boris Yeltsin in a runoff against the communist challenger Gennady Zyuganov, Lebed, a 46-year-old former army two-star general, became overnight one of that country's most powerful men. Despite his expected failure to place as a finalist himself, Lebed nevertheless became Russia's man of the hour with a surprisingly strong finish in third place. That positioned him as a kingmaker to swing the July 3 runoff between the two top contenders and prompted a scramble by both finalists to garner his support.

Once it had become clear that Yeltsin had a straight shot at reelection, he enlisted Lebed as his national security adviser and Security Council secretary in a masterstroke of cooptation. He also went so far as to intimate, at least once, that he might also be grooming Lebed to be his successor as president. However well or poorly Lebed fares in his new assignment, his youth and dynamism, his popularity among Russia's have-nots, and his consuming ambition all suggest that he is likely to remain a prominent player in Russian politics for some time. Accordingly, it is important for Western military and defense leaders to understand who he really is and what he represents.

Until his recent rise to a position of prominence, the dominant tendency of the Western press was to treat Lebed as a curiosity, portraying him in terms that dwelt mainly on his flamboyance and seeming uniqueness. While accurate as far as it went, that image was informed more by anecdotes and sound bites than by deeper inquiry into what Lebed actually had to say. In the process, it masked a more multifaceted character underneath. Especially since he has assumed his new role as Yeltsin's chief security aide, he has been uninhibited in his public pronouncements and in interviews with reporters. Close examination of these reveals a persona both deeper and more balanced than the prevalent two-dimensional image purveyed by most media accounts. Now that Lebed's power is real, what does his presence on the scene imply for Russia and for broader East-West relations?

Lebed's domestic agenda will focus on four key problem areas: (1) crime and corruption, (2) the war in Chechnya, (3) the composition and role of the Security Council, and (4) military reform. With respect to the first of these, assuming that he does not self-destruct through his own missteps or otherwise become consumed by Kremlin intrigue, Lebed can be expected to try to lend real teeth to the police and to crack down on Soviet captains of industry who have become rich at the expense of the rank and file.

As for the war in Chechnya, Lebed was recently delivered a golden opportunity to make good on his campaign pledge to negotiate a settlement that will stop the killing and allow both sides to emerge with honor. On August 6, rebel forces counterattacked in strength and retook the capital city of Grozny within days. That launched Lebed on a three-week roller coaster ride of shuttle diplomacy with the rebel commander, General Aslan Maskhadov, and high-stakes politics with both his army peers and Yeltsin's chief lieutenants in Moscow. As this report goes to press, Lebed has concluded a framework agreement with the Chechen resistance that, for the first time in 20 months of war, has produced a genuinely promising end to the conflict and has postponed a final ruling on the status of the contested Russian republic until December 31, 2001.

This achievement, however, has elicited at best only lukewarm support from President Yeltsin. It has also occasioned a studied distancing act by Yeltsin's principal deputies, feeding well-founded suspicions in both Moscow and the West that Lebed is being set up by his detractors for a massive fall. Nevertheless, thanks to his prodigious efforts to date, he has made the war in Chechnya Yeltsin's alone to lose. Either way, Lebed stands well-positioned on the high ground, with the equally serviceable options of resigning on principle should Yeltsin fail to support the peace process, or else charging betrayal by a two-timing and duplicitous Yeltsin administration should he eventually be sent packing for having exceeded his charter. One thing, of course, that could undo all this for Lebed—quickly and perhaps disastrously—would be for rebel forces to renege on their declared commitment to peace with a semblance of honor for Russia and resume fighting for total stakes, thus allowing Yeltsin to make a scapegoat of Lebed and jettison him for cause for having been snookered by the enemy. Even that, however, would probably not signal an end to Lebed's political career for the longer haul given the depth of his commitment and the strength of his electoral constituency.

The Security Council under Lebed's tutelage will almost certainly play a more influential role in Russia's defense and security policy-making, if only because of the power and magnetism of Lebed's personality. He has left no room for doubt that he is seeking a broadened mandate as Russia's chief security planner. The prospect of his Security Council becoming a bureaucratic juggernaut, however, should not be overstated. The Russian security policy apparatus remains poorly institutionalized, and personal rivals of Lebed's have already begun building political alliances and forming counterbalances.

Military reform is Lebed's strongest suit, as well as the policy issue on which his public statements have been most detailed and on which he has the greatest chance of making real progress. Where personnel matters are concerned, he has vowed that important posts will no longer be filled by "good old boys," but rather by professionals who can meet the objective test of competence. Lebed also may seek to depoliticize the armed forces through legislation. He has been adamant in insisting that the military's sole reason for existing is to protect the country against external aggression, not to take sides in domestic disputes. Beyond that, he will strive to end draft evasion by sons of the well-to-do, on the premise that conscription must gather the best of Russia's youth. He maintains that an all-volunteer military entails costs reaching well beyond Russia's grasp, and he has expressed doubts about the feasibility of Yeltsin's campaign promise to end the draft and create a professional army by the year 2000.

Lebed has often stressed that the Russian military needs to get rid of its many separate channels for reporting up the chain of command. He has repeatedly charged that the country's debacle in Chechnya was partly the result of a compartmentalized military organizational structure at all levels, which caused the right hand all too often not to know what the left was doing. He also advocates eliminating skeleton divisions, and he has declared that he will propose to Yeltsin that the latter should announce that the military in 1997-1998 will abandon its current practice of maintaining undermanned units. Those units having only 25–30 percent of the required manning level would be converted into storage bases.

Lebed has promised to reduce the Russian armed forces by a third. He has called for a new three-tiered army structure consisting of airborne forces and specially trained general-purpose forces at level one; fully manned infantry and armored formations with appropriate equipment and munitions at level two; and bases, storage facilities, and logistic structures at level three. He will probably stick with the existing five-service arrangement for the time being. He will also probably pursue reform measures that focus on building a healthy military institution before seeking to acquire new hardware for its own sake. He will press hard at the same time—to the extent possible under Russia's continuing cash shortage—for increased allocations to defense. In addition, he will strive to resurrect the military industry.

Internationally, Lebed can be expected to leave his mark primarily in three areas: (1) Russia's security strategy, (2) the disposition of tensions in the so-called "near abroad" (the other former Soviet republics), and (3) Russia's response to NATO enlargement. On the first count, Lebed has announced that the conceptual framework for a new Russian approach to security already exists and that the challenge is to establish a mechanism for its implementation. However that pans out, the odds are scant that he will seek to pursue an expansionist policy beyond the borders of the former Soviet Union. More than any other nationalist contender for president, he understands that Russia lacks the wherewithal to pursue such a strategy, even were it deemed to be attractive in principle. Lebed's main concern is that Russia regain its self-respect and be taken seriously around the world. He has cited Russia's marginalization in the Yugoslav crisis as an example of what can happen when a once-great power loses its former clout.

Lebed freely admits that the USSR lost the cold war because of the failed policies of the communists. Accordingly, he will not be inclined to seek a settling of old scores with the United States and NATO. Lebed is not a jingoist, and he has taken a firm stance against organizations supporting fascism. He will take a strong lead, however, in nurturing the development and articulation of a security concept for Russia that reasserts Russia's status as a global power, short of confrontation with the West.

As for the "near abroad," Lebed feels strong compulsions to see to the social and political protection of the 25 million Russians living in the former Soviet republics. It is unlikely, however, that he will advocate outright coercion toward that end or pursue lesser means that blatantly violate the sovereignty of the newly independent states. Lebed has admitted that economic integration out of mutual self-interest and a possible confederation among consenting former republics constitute the outer limits of any acceptable Russian effort to put Humpty Dumpty back together again.

Lebed can be expected, however, to argue for firm steps against any eastward NATO expansion that does not make a satisfactory offsetting provision for Russia's security concerns and sense of being first among equals in Central Europe. This should come as no surprise to the West. Lebed's earlier declared views on NATO enlargement were more blustery than many. But at bottom his perspective on the issue remains quintessentially mainstream. Since his appointment as Yeltsin's security adviser, he has shown indications of being less adamant over this divisive issue than most policy elites in Moscow, an encouraging sign that he may be acquiring a more pragmatic policy outlook. In pursuing this new line, Lebed has adopted a clever stance. Rather than being frontally critical of NATO enlargement, he has asked the United States and its allies, in effect: "Have you really thought this through?" That does not mean that he has become indifferent to NATO expansion. It merely testifies to his status as the first senior establishment figure in Moscow to acknowledge Russia's limited ability, at least today, to do much about it—beyond complaining.

Lebed has voiced skepticism over Partnership for Peace, NATO's arrangement for engaging the military establishments of the former Warsaw Pact states, including Russia. This may merely reflect his lack of much first-hand exposure to the West. Insofar as that may be the case, it points up a problem that should be remediable through astute NATO initiatives aimed at engaging him constructively. One concern that might incline Lebed to think hard about the merits of a security relationship with the West is his evident unease over China's ambitions and long-term strategic prospects.

It will be interesting to see whether Lebed will succeed in enduring for long the petty humiliations and daily hassles that are the inevitable lot of a civilian bureaucratic politician. As an army general, Lebed had grown accustomed to having things his way. He will need to develop new expectations and habit patterns if he is to survive in his new incarnation. If Lebed can control his ambitions, remain directed and focused, and play to his greatest professional strengths, he has every chance of gaining credibility as a politician and building a foundation for bigger things to come. This will necessarily mean concentrating on those issues where he can make a real difference and avoiding the squandering of his energy on needless turf wars. On the positive side, to cite just one example, Lebed could serve as a counterweight to the tendency of Yevgeny Primakov's foreign ministry to cozy up to troublesome countries like China and Iran.

As for relations with the United States, there is no reason for Washington to assume the worst from Lebed's recent rise to a position of policymaking influence. Despite some early sharp flashes over the NATO expansion issue and his disdain for what he regards as debased American values, Lebed has shown little sign of an ingrained animus toward the West that would predispose him to confrontational conduct. Depending on how we in the West approach him, we may find in him either an antagonist or a businesslike, if sometimes difficult, workmate in security affairs.

Of course, Lebed, having often stressed the importance of Russia's nuclear posture as the nation's last line of defense, could prove nettlesome with respect to the stalled ratification of the START II Treaty. Other areas where he may prove prickly could include the question of arms sales to pariah states and the possibility that he might support a turn to reactionary policies at home.

That said, Lebed has admitted that Russia has little choice but to engage the West. He has also granted that the West has much to offer toward helping integrate Russia into the world as an accepted power. There is no prima facie reason to believe that he will oppose continued, and even expanded, military contacts with the United States. American defense leaders should test him on this as soon as possible.

All in all, the United States has nothing to lose and perhaps much to gain by reaching out to involve Lebed in an effort to build a mature Russian-American relationship shorn of romantic expectations. For better or for worse, his success story to date reflects the voice of the Russian people. It also reflects Russia's ongoing struggle to transform itself into a rule-of-law state. If the United States is properly solicitous and inclined to engage the shaky new Yeltsin government without the patronizing overlay that has hitherto often triggered bad feelings among Russians of all persuasions, Lebed may well be disposed to respond in kind. If we in the West write him off too soon as a man on horseback who threatens all we have hoped for in Russian reform, however, we could contribute to a self-fulfilling prophecy and live to regret it.

ACKNOWLEDGMENTS

For their helpful comments on several earlier versions of this report, I am grateful to Colonel Roger Bort, USA, Office of the Deputy Assistant Secretary of Defense for Russia and Eurasia; Colonel David Glantz, USA (Ret.), editor of the *Journal of Slavic Military Studies*; James F. Hoge, Jr., Council on Foreign Relations; Fred Charles Iklé, Center for Strategic and International Studies; Jacob Kipp and Timothy Thomas, U.S. Army Foreign Military Studies Office; Charles William Maynes, Carnegie Endowment for International Peace; and my RAND colleagues Jeremy Azrael, Abraham Becker, Carl Builder, Harry Gelman, Jerrold Green, Arnold Horelick, Zalmay Khalilzad, Robert Nurick, William O'Malley, and John Van Oudenaren. I also wish to note a word of thanks to my editor, Malcolm Palmatier.

ABBREVIATIONS

CIA	Central Intelligence Agency
CNN	Cable News Network
CPSU	Communist Party of the Soviet Union
CSCE	Conference on Security and Cooperation in Europe
FSB	Russian Federal Security Service
KGB	Soviet Committee for State Security
KRO	Congress of Russian Communities
MPA	Main Political Administration
MVD	Russian Ministry of Internal Affairs
NATO	North Atlantic Treaty Organization
NTV	Russian Independent Television Network
START	Strategic Arms Reduction Treaty
USAF	United States Air Force
USSR	Union of Soviet Socialist Republics
VTsIOM	All-Russian Center for the Study of Public Opinion

"I have already stopped one war."

Aleksandr I. Lebed's Presidential Election Campaign Poster

Chapter One

INTRODUCTION

Following Russia's presidential election on June 16, 1996, which placed Boris Yeltsin in a runoff against the communist Gennady Zyuganov, Aleksandr I. Lebed became, literally overnight, one of that country's most powerful men. He further confirmed himself, in the words of one American editorial comment, to be "supremely confident and undisguisedly ambitious."[1] Buoyed by his own surprisingly strong third-place showing in the first round of the election, with 15 percent of the vote to Yeltsin's 35 percent and Zyuganov's 32 percent, he declared himself a "born winner" whose "time has not yet come."[2] The following day, thanks to his newly acquired leverage as kingmaker for the subsequent runoff on July 3 that ultimately returned Yeltsin to office, he was formally enlisted by Yeltsin to be the latter's security adviser, Security Council chief, and even, or so it seemed for the moment, heir apparent.[3]

The 46-year-old former army two-star general had enjoyed a swift rise in popularity during the preceding two years owing to his strong stands against crime, corruption, and the Yeltsin government's military quagmire in Chechnya. For a time, given his charismatic appeal among Russia's dispossessed and his frequently stated determination to help right the country's wrongs, he was widely assumed to be

---

[1] "The Mixed Blessing of Lebed," *Los Angeles Times*, June 20, 1996.

[2] Interview on Moscow NTV, June 16, 1996.

[3] For one of the first predictions by anyone that the Russian president would pull off such a remarkable recovery despite his abysmal approval ratings and doubtful prospects at the end of 1995, see Alex Alexiev, "Yeltsin Looking More Like the Comeback Kid," *Los Angeles Times*, January 21, 1996.

the challenger primed to unseat Yeltsin in the gathering presidential showdown. After the failure of his party to gain the 5 percent of the vote needed to secure a place for itself in the state Duma (lower house of the Russian parliament) last December, however, it appeared that his presidential prospects had fizzled. In a statement that neatly summed up most Western opinion in the wake of his party's poor showing in the December election, the authoritative London *Economist* wrote him off as a "busted flush."[4]

Nevertheless, Lebed won a seat for himself in the Duma as an independent and went on to reaffirm his intent to run for president. During the early months of the campaign, he lagged so far behind in the polling that he was all but forgotten in Western reporting. He did not, however, drop off the political radar screen entirely.[5] In late January, he declared that he would withdraw from the race altogether if that would help another candidate who showed real promise of uniting all forces in wresting power from the hands of what he called the Yeltsinite "pseudo-reformers."[6]

For their part, the leading contenders among the reform democrats were eager to draw strength from Lebed's sources of support. One early report cited talk in Moscow of "a reformers' coalition with Lebed, who is anti-communist and anti-Yeltsin, and might find attractive the defense ministry and later a reconstituted vice presidency."[7] Even Mikhail Gorbachev, who was vainly pursuing a second chance of his own at national leadership despite his almost unanimous rejection by Russia's electorate as a spent force, more recently intimated that Lebed would be well suited to serve on a "democratic team" because he is "a man capable of doing something in the military sphere."[8]

---

[4]"The Devil They Don't Know," *The Economist* (London), December 23, 1995, p. 61.

[5]A poll of 1361 voters taken by the Public Opinion Fund in late January, asking who they would choose for president if the election were held at that time, gave Zyuganov 17 percent, Yavlinsky 11 percent, Yeltsin 10 percent, Zhirinovsky 8.9 percent, and Lebed 8.5 percent. See Claudia Rosett and Steve Liesman, "Yeltsin, Zyuganov Join Race for Russian Presidency," *Wall Street Journal*, February 16, 1996.

[6]Interfax, Moscow, January 24, 1996.

[7]William Safire, "Who's Losing Russia?" *New York Times*, February 8, 1996.

[8]Information Agency *Ekho Moskvy*, March 9, 1996. In reply, Lebed was less charitable, commenting after the election that "Mikhail Sergeyevich wanted very much to be my

In the ensuing months, Lebed became involved in dealings with the principal democratic challenger, Grigory Yavlinsky, and renowned ophthalmologist and popular parliamentarian Svyatoslav Fyodorov, over the tantalizing idea of forming a "Third Force" that might have a chance of edging Yeltsin out in quest of a runoff against Zyuganov.[9] That move was prompted by a growing realization among all three contenders of the vote-getting potential of a centrist alternative to Yeltsin and Zyuganov. It remained stalled to the bitter end, however, by an inability of the three to decide who among them should take the lead.[10] That left Lebed to take on the two front-running candidates by himself, on the strength of little more than his name recognition and his reputation for incorruptibility. Said Leonid Radzhikovskii, one of his key campaign advisers, Lebed pressed ahead in the presidential sweepstakes in the end "like a gambler with only 10 rubles left, who could either buy a sandwich or stake it all at the casino."[11]

Despite his failure to place as a finalist in the June 16 presidential election, Lebed became Russia's man of the hour as a result of his unexpectedly solid emergence in third place. That positioned him to swing the July 3 runoff between the two top contenders and prompted a scramble by both finalists to garner his support. Earlier, Yeltsin had shamelessly courted his one-time nemesis, reportedly offering Lebed the position of defense minister and providing more than $1 million in support to his campaign to draw votes from Zyuganov. Once it had become clear that Yeltsin had a straight shot at reelection in the July runoff, he enlisted Lebed as his national security adviser and Security Council secretary in a masterstroke of cooptation. He also went so far as to intimate at least once that he

---

daddy. I preferred to remain an orphan." Quoted in Jonas Bernstein, "Run, Gorby, Run!" *The American Spectator*, July 1996, p. 60. Not to be outdone, Gorbachev evinced a trace of sour grapes following the election when he commented on Lebed's cooptation by Yeltsin: "I used to have a fairly positive view of Lebed, but I was astonished by his behavior during the election when he failed to join forces with other centrist candidates." Mikhail Gorbachev, "Will Alexander Lebed Be the Napoleon of Russia's Election?" *Boston Globe*, July 3, 1996.

[9]Nikolai Dolgopolov, "'Third Force' Currently Divided Between Three," *Komsomolskaia pravda*, March 21, 1996.

[10]See Claudia Rosett, "'Third Force' Stumbles in Russian Race," *Wall Street Journal*, April 1, 1996.

[11]Lee Hockstader, "Lebed's Meteoric Ascent," *Washington Post*, June 25, 1996.

might be considering grooming Lebed to be his successor as Russia's president. By one account, Lebed's rise from the ranks of the also-rans to the status of a Moscow heavyweight within just days may go down in Russian history as "the most unlikely since an eccentric village priest named Rasputin was once elevated to the court of Tsar Nicholas II."[12] Among other things, it almost instantly made Lebed a man with whom the U.S. government will have to contend on such matters as NATO enlargement, Russia's role in NATO's Partnership for Peace, strategic arms reduction, and Russian-American security relations.

However well or poorly he fares in his new assignment in the short run, Lebed's youth and dynamism, his popularity among Russia's have-nots, and his consuming ambition all suggest that will remain a prominent player in Russian politics for some time. Accordingly, it is essential that American and allied military and defense leaders understand, insofar as possible, who he really is and what he represents. A clearer sense of what Lebed stands for with respect to the imperatives of Russian security policy can take Western decision-makers considerably beyond the realm of pure guesswork as to the outlook for Russia's international conduct over the coming decade. Alternative scenarios offered for Russia's future development have ranged from continued, if halting, progress toward domestic reform and constructive engagement with the West to a rise of angry irredentism and undisciplined nuclear threatsmanship that could make Western leaders yearn for the more predictable days of the cold war. Between these polar opposites, a Russia that marches to the drumbeat of Lebed's vision and values will be both a more forceful presence in world affairs and a more demanding challenge to Western diplomacy than has been the government of Boris Yeltsin to date. But it will not, by any measure, represent the worst case for the West.

Based on the extensive record of his political and philosophical outlook to date, this report documents that assertion by reviewing the highlights of Lebed's background, outlining his views on the key issues confronting Russia, and indicating what his recent rise to influ-

---

[12]Ibid.

ence and future leadership may portend for Russia and the West.[13] Although he remains as yet only at the edge of commanding real power in Moscow, Lebed stands as an almost classic prototype of the newly emerging breed of proud but disciplined Russian nationalist with whom the United States is going to have to deal now that earlier hopes for a speedy reformation of its former cold war rival have been proven premature. Until recently, he drew Western interest because he was an insubordinate general with exceptional ambition and popular appeal. Today, he demands attention in the West because he has attained a position of real policy influence and has become, more than ever before, a credible contender for national leadership. The near-term prospect for a range of countries, Russia included, is ambiguity: leaderships that are neither friends nor enemies, and governments that are neither classically democratic nor systemically totalitarian. Lebed neatly defines at least one category of a post-cold war leadership type that does not readily fit the categories that have served us in the West so conveniently in the past. That fact alone makes it important for us to "go to school" on him.[14]

---

[13]Late last year, Lebed published a memoir nearly 500 pages long entitled *Za derzhavu obidno. . .* ("It Is a Pity for a Great Power . . . ") Moscow, "Gregori-Peidzh," publishing house of the newspaper *Moskovskaia pravda,* 1995. That volume, in effect Lebed's campaign autobiography, largely contains personal reflections and reminiscences rather than any focused political or strategic vision. For an insightful first-look assessment of the book, see Jacob W. Kipp, "The Political Ballet of General Aleksandr Ivanovich Lebed: Implications for Russia's Presidential Elections," *Problems of Post-Communism,* July–August 1996, pp. 43–53.

[14]I am indebted to my RAND colleague John Van Oudenaren for sharing this point with me.

Chapter Two

THE POPULAR IMAGE OF LEBED

Since he first came on the scene more than two years ago as the feisty commander of Russia's 14th Army in Moldova, Lebed has often been portrayed as a would-be Douglas MacArthur—or even a Napoleon. Those closest to him, physically and in spirit, have spoken of him reverentially as Russia's only hope. His own former executive assistant, Colonel Mikhail Bergman, extolled him as "a new Peter the Great" and "a personality of cosmic dimensions" on a vector to become "Russia's next president."[1] A senior writer for the military's daily paper, *Krasnaia zvezda*, likewise declared that Lebed is "destined to reach the summit of Russia's Olympus."[2] As a measure of his credibility, he is reputed to have been the best battalion commander in the Soviet army. He is also said to have been the only Russian general respected by the Chechen irregulars.

Until his recent rise to a position of importance, the Western press tended to treat Lebed as a curiosity, portraying him in terms that dwelt mainly on his flamboyance and seeming uniqueness. A typical characterization depicted him as "a commodity that cynical post-communist Russia has in short supply—a hero" and as "the spiritual leader of the army, as the Rambo who would not abandon brethren caught on the perilous outskirts of the old empire."[3] Others have

---

[1] "Aide Warns of 'Plot' to Oust Top Russian General," Reuters dispatch, August 9, 1994.

[2] Ibid.

[3] Carey Goldberg, "Army Hero Is Many Russians' Fantasy Leader," *Los Angeles Times*, January 9, 1995.

spoken loosely of his "macho populism."[4] He has been called "gruff, honest, authoritarian in style, yet relatively moderate in his politics," with a voice so deep and reverberating ("its rumble has been compared to cannon fire") that television sound engineers cannot get decent audio quality in his office.[5] The most thorough and analytically detached appraisal of him to date called him "Russia's most popular leader, appreciated as being professional and uncorrupted."[6]

This image of Lebed, while fair and accurate as far as it goes, has for the most part been informed by anecdotes and sound bites rather than by deeper inquiry into what he has actually had to say or who he is. It focuses to a fault on his remarkable gift for colorful expression on virtually any topic of concern in Russia today. In the process it masks a more multifaceted character underneath. As Charles William Maynes, the editor of *Foreign Policy*, succinctly puts it: "Western coverage of [Lebed] has been terrible. We are looking for a monster and he has the misfortune to wander on the scene at the wrong moment. Yet when one looks carefully at what he says, as only a few have done, it is not necessarily bad."[7]

In a nutshell, Lebed is more than the simple rough-riding hussar that a scan of his pithy one-liners might suggest. (For a selection of some of the richer examples, see "A Sampler of Lebedisms" appended at the end of this report.) Especially since he became a leading critic of the war in Chechnya and began openly dabbling in politics in early 1995, Lebed has been uninhibited in his interviews with reporters. Close examination of these reveals a persona far deeper and more balanced than the prevalent two-dimensional image purveyed by most media treatments. As Yeltsin's former security adviser Yury Baturin pointed out in reply to a newspaper editor's question on just

---

[4]Alessandra Stanley, "Russian General Woos Votes for Old-Time Soviet Values," *New York Times*, October 13, 1995.

[5]Steven Erlanger, "Yeltsin Allows Critic in Army to Quit Post," *New York Times*, June 15, 1995, and Goldberg, *Los Angeles Times*, January 9, 1995.

[6]S. G. Simonson, "Going His Own Way: A Profile of General Aleksandr Lebed," *The Journal of Slavic Military Studies*, September 1995, p. 528. This excellent portrait of Lebed concentrates on his tenure as 14th Army commander in Moldova. Unfortunately, its information cutoff date occurred just as Lebed's public persona was beginning to emerge into full bloom. The present study continues where Simonson's article leaves off.

[7]Letter to the author, January 22, 1996.

this point, he is a man who has "little in common with his TV image."[8] In one of the first American press acknowledgments of this point, the *Washington Post* rightly observed shortly after the June 16 election that Lebed "has shown himself to be more than the caricature of a would-be military dictator that his detractors draw."[9]

Although he is far from having the stature of a soldier-statesman like retired U.S. Army General Colin Powell, Lebed is no chauvinist of Vladimir Zhirinovsky's ilk. The suggestion that on reviewing his writings, "the fine distinctions between Lebed and Zhirinovsky begin to disappear"[10] is simply wrong. A bona fide military professional, he is not even remotely of a piece with what the late Soviet premier Nikita Khrushchev once disparaged as "those thick-headed types you find wearing uniforms." He is said to love classical music and to quote Goethe and Schiller—although one might give such reports the same weight as the similar hagiography portraying former KGB head and, for a time, Brezhnev successor Yury Andropov in 1982 as a scotch-sipping, jazz-loving closet liberal who portended major reforms for the Soviet Union.[11]

Nor is Lebed an ideologue eager to exploit popular unrest for an opportunity to turn the clock back, reestablish totalitarian rule, and recommit Russia to a long-term competition for global hegemony. Rather, he is an avowed patriot who has sought to present himself as a bastion of civic rectitude at a time when everything he has grown up to believe in has progressively unravelled during the four years since the USSR's demise. Consistent with this cultivated image of high standards of personal conduct, he has forsworn alcohol on the

---

[8]Interview with editor-in-chief Vitaly Tretyakov, "Yury Baturin Learned About His Resignation from the President Himself. Boris Yeltsin Asked Him to Stay On for Another Month to Hand Business Over to Aleksandr Lebed," *Nezavisimaia gazeta*, June 20, 1996.

[9]"General Lebed's Ascent," *Washington Post*, June 20, 1996.

[10]Alan J. Koman, "Princes of Darkness," *Armed Forces Journal International*, January 1996, p. 11.

[11]More recently, Lebed has revealed a penchant for the 19th-century Russian satirists Nikolai Gogol and Mikhail Soltykov-Shchedrin, as well as for Somerset Maugham as a foreign favorite. See "Lebedtime Reading," *The Economist* (London), July 27, 1996, p. 43.

stated premise that "at least one person in the country should be sober."[12]

At bottom, Lebed has shown little sign that he is fundamentally anti-reform. Nor is there evidence that he is anti-West in principle. True, he has voiced opposition to the idea of NATO expansion. But that view is shared by everyone in Russia. More recently, he has given indications that he may be less hard over on this divisive issue in East-West relations than most policy elites in Moscow.

At his core, Lebed is a champion of social order. His constant harping against organized crime and government corruption has made him almost a prototypical answer to the prayers of the disaffected man on the street, whose most pained cry of late has been for *vlast i distsiplina* ("power and discipline") to check the gathering forces of decadence and disarray in Russia.

More important, Lebed has built up an immense popularity within the ranks. Three-quarters of the academy cadets polled in August 1994 preferred him as their choice for defense minister. (None voiced support for the recently dismissed incumbent, General Grachev.)[13] That same year, in the widely publicized Friedrich Ebert Foundation poll of 615 Russian officers, including 60 generals and admirals, Lebed and General Boris Gromov were the only two figures to achieve higher than a 50-percent rating on a question of whom the respondents trusted most, and to score lower than 20 percent on a disapproval rating.[14] By contrast, Grachev scored only 20 percent, with a 50-percent disapproval rating.[15]

---

[12]Henriette Schroeder, "At Least One Person Should Be Sober," *Suddeutsche Zeitung* (Munich), February 4–5, 1995.

[13]"Lebed Emerges as Possible Major Player in Russian Politics," Associated Press dispatch, August 11, 1994, reporting the results of a poll published in the Moscow daily, *Segodnya*.

[14]One account in a right-wing Moscow newspaper cited a new divide at the top of the military leadership between the "aggrieved principals," headed by Gromov and including Lebed and airborne commander Colonel General Yevgeny Podkolzin; the "cautiously grumbling generals," led by the chief of the General Staff, Army General Mikhail Kolesnikov; and the "October 1993 generals," led by Grachev. See "Scoreboard," *Zavtra*, No. 2, January 1995, p. 1.

[15]John Lloyd, "Russian Military in Troubled Mood," *Financial Times* (London), September 8, 1994.

A MODERN BONAPARTE?

Lebed's strong following and his sense of being the military's anointed savior from the depredations of Soviet communism and Yeltsin's misrule raise a natural question for the continued prospect of military subordination to civil authority in Russian politics. Stanford University Slavic expert Gregory Friedin has underscored Lebed's "powerful sense of mission," noting that the maverick former general was raised not in the Communist Party's "snake pits," but rather in a service branch that nurtured genuine leadership and such "patently non-Soviet personal and social skills" as individual initiative, honor, adaptability, and the ability to take responsibility.[16] Does this mean that Lebed's rise to political influence and the possibility of his replacing Yeltsin within the next four years presage a militarization of Russian politics?

Throughout the history of Soviet civil-military relations, an abiding concern of the communists was to contain what was felt to be a danger of "Bonapartism" lurking within the High Command. Such concern was a major underlying reason for establishment of the Main Political Administration (MPA), the Communist Party's mechanism for ensuring political control of the Soviet armed forces.

That organization was hated by most officers of all ranks, who saw it as antithetical to good training and an affront to their professionalism. When the USSR collapsed in 1991, one of the first steps of the new Russian defense ministry was to disestablish the MPA. Defense minister Yevgeny Shaposhnikov stated that the military could be counted on to police itself, because it had no interest in political involvement.[17] However, Lebed's subsequent rise in popularity and his open aspirations to higher leadership lead one to wonder whether he may be, in effect, a warrior waiting in the wings.

With the unfulfilled promise of reform in Russia and the predictable rise in appeals to nationalism as a result, it was only a matter of time before the military would become susceptible to the tugging and

---

[16]Gregory Friedin, "Wishing the 'Swan' Well in His Mission," *Los Angeles Times*, June 23, 1996. The name "Lebed" translates into English as "swan."

[17]For further discussion, see Benjamin S. Lambeth, *Russia's Air Power at the Crossroads*, Santa Monica, California, RAND, MR-623-AF, 1996, pp. 14–16.

hauling of those contenders who would court its favor. Because of his outrageous views and erratic style, the tendency among most Westerners and Russians alike has been to dismiss the right-wing extremist Vladimir Zhirinovsky as a harmless buffoon and an unlikely suitor. Thoughtful observers, however, have spotlighted the chauvinist forces that prompted Zhirinovsky's success in the December 1993 parliamentary election and have cautioned that they deserve the West's attention and respect. The concern here was not that Zhirinovsky might arise to lead Russia, but that he could be the pathbreaker for a contender of like sentiment, yet with greater sophistication, self-discipline, and political directedness—and possibly wearing shoulderboards. As William Pfaff put it: "The danger is not Zhirinovsky. It is that he has opened the way for a serious nationalism, a truly anti-Western and pan-Slavic movement. . . . Vladimir Zhirinovsky is merely a clown. But the clown leads in a parade in which lions and tigers and elephants, freaks and monsters, may in turn follow."[18]

It is thus a valid question whether Lebed might be the prototype of such a contender, if not the figure who could actually make this grim prophecy come true. Obviously disquieted at such a possibility, the Moscow newspaper *Kuranty* early on likened him to the screen actor Arnold Schwarzenegger and called him "a Russian Terminator," confessing frankly that "we are afraid of Lebed. We fear that we may easily find ourselves not protected but smashed by his enormous fists."[19] The charismatic former general has resonated with the dark mood of an embittered populace sick of crime and corruption, inclined toward aggressive rhetoric, and, in the words of one observer, "drawn to the appeal of a mythical former glory and idealized imperial past."[20]

Time will tell whether Lebed is a populist on the surface with something more substantial underneath or merely a hollow shell with an appealing message and an engaging personal style. Either way, how-

---

[18]William Pfaff, "The Winner: A Monster Made in the West," *Los Angeles Times*, December 15, 1993.

[19]Quoted in Sonni Efron, "Popular Russian General Quits; May Run Against Yeltsin in '96," *Los Angeles Times*, June 2, 1995.

[20]Adrian Karatnycky, "Communism Gone, Russia Goes Bonkers," *Wall Street Journal*, May 9, 1995.

ever, now that he has hung up his uniform, any portrayal of him as a potential Bonaparte has been rendered moot. This does *not* mean that Lebed would not bring disturbing martial values, and perhaps even a militarist orientation, to the Kremlin were he to succeed Yeltsin as president. Yet such an occurrence would no more entail a military encroachment into politics than would General Colin Powell's putative pursuit of the American presidency, should he ultimately elect to throw his hat into the ring.

Chapter Three

LEBED'S RISE TO PUBLIC PROMINENCE

Aleksandr Ivanovich Lebed was born on April 20, 1950 to working-class parents in the town of Novocherkassk, located in a Cossack area in the Rostov Oblast of southern Russia. As a high school student, he applied three times for admission to the Soviet Air Defense Force's Armavir flight school for training as an interceptor pilot—but without success, owing to a failure to qualify in the medical exams. He finally graduated as an army lieutenant from the Ryazan Higher Airborne Forces School and later commanded the first battalion of the 345th Airborne Regiment in Afghanistan, where he earned the Order of the Red Star on combat assignment in 1981–1982. He subsequently completed his senior service school education at the Frunze Academy and went on to command the Tula airborne division from 1985 to 1991, at which time he was appointed deputy commander of airborne forces following the failed August coup.

Lebed first gained public attention when, as commander of the Tula division, he balked at supporting the August 1991 coup plotters and came instead to the defense of Boris Yeltsin. He remarked at the time that any use of military force in the streets of Moscow "would have been guaranteed 100 percent to lead to large-scale bloodshed," which would have "engulfed the country in civil war," something it was "imperative to prevent."[1]

This loyalty to Yeltsin was duly noted by defense minister Grachev, who selected Lebed the following year to command the Russian 14th

---

[1]"Anti-Coup Leaders: The Men of the Future?" *Jane's Intelligence Review*, October 1991.

Army in newly independent Moldova. Lebed arrived at a time of escalating tension between the government of Moldova and the rump Transdniester Russian Republic. Populated mostly by Russians and Ukrainians, the Dniester region had declared its autonomy from Moldova in response to an upsurge of Moldovan nationalism against the Russian minority. An ensuing conflict simmered for weeks and finally broke out into open fighting that killed hundreds.[2]

Moscow had ordered Lebed to stay neutral. Lebed, however, declared defiantly that "there come times when you must not chatter but act. Everybody agreed that it was a wild, stupid war that could lead nowhere. . . . So I decided to put an end to it firmly and resolutely." Lebed's troops unleashed such an artillery barrage on the Moldovans who were advancing on Tiraspol, the capital of the self-proclaimed Russian republic, that the latter were forced to retreat. That action cast Lebed as a wildcat who refused to be bound by Moscow's preferences with respect to Russia's so-called "near abroad." It carried the day for his Russian compatriots in Moldova.[3]

In effect, Lebed privatized the 14th Army. In so doing, he boldly assumed a stance of independence from his superiors in Moscow. As he stated in an early interview, "theoretically we are under the orders of the commander in chief of the Ground Forces in Moscow. In practice, we make decisions here."[4] To be sure, Lebed was no apologist for the Transdniester regime. His sole concern was for the proper treatment of the Russian minority living in Moldova. Indeed, long after the initial tension had subsided, Lebed declared that he no longer had any interest in the "thoroughly false and criminal organ" that had turned the Dniester region into a "zone of irresponsibility." He explained that the mafia reigned supreme there because the titu-

---

[2]For a well-informed treatment of the events leading up to and surrounding this unpleasantness, see Irina Selivanova, "Russia's Policy in the Transdniester Conflict: The Problems of the 14th Army," paper prepared for a conference on U.S. and Russian Policymaking with Respect to the Use of Force, jointly sponsored by RAND's Center for Russian and Eurasian Studies and the Russian Center for Ethnopolitical and Regional Studies, Washington, D.C., September 27–28, 1995.

[3]Carey Goldberg, *Los Angeles Times*, January 9, 1995.

[4]"The Threat That Was," *The Economist* (London), August 28, 1993, p. 17.

lar head of the Transdniester Russian Republic was always "either drunk or off hunting."[5]

Nevertheless, Lebed was far more than an assertive general who took liberties with his position in Moldova. He was manifestly insubordinate, not only to his superiors in the defense ministry but also to his commander in chief, President Yeltsin. In point of fact, he was uncontrollable and frequently went out of his way to cultivate such an image, on one occasion declaring dramatically: "Don't touch me or the families of my officers, and I'll do nothing to you. Touch me, and I'll hit you—hard."[6]   This tendency toward headstrong independence and his inclination to disobey higher authority whenever motivated by his personal sense of right and wrong raise a warning flag regarding the example Lebed may set for Russia's armed forces now that he has a hand in security policymaking. However much distaste Americans may have felt for Grachev's policies toward Chechnya and military corruption, at least he strongly endorsed the principle of military subordination to civilian authority. By contrast, Lebed's truculent defiance of Moscow while he was 14th Army commander in Moldova reflects an attitude regarding compliance with the will of his superiors that is ambiguous at best.

FROM PROFESSIONAL SOLDIER TO POPULIST POLITICIAN

Lebed's image as a go-it-alone maverick assumed its initial form in the wake of his assertive moves to protect the Russian minority in Moldova. He only peaked as a defiant general with ambitions beyond surviving the disapprobation of his superiors, however, with the onset of Russian combat operations in Chechnya. Once that threshold was crossed, he became an outspoken critic of Grachev and Yeltsin, going so far as to characterize Yeltsin as "useless" and adding that "a president under the influence is no longer the president. He is failing in his first duty, which is to guarantee the country's stability."[7]

---

[5] Interview by Vitaly Knyazev, "General Lebed: A Cat When Backed into a Corner Becomes a Tiger," *Sobesednik*, No. 16, April 1995, p. 3.

[6] *The Economist* (London), August 28, 1993, p. 17.

[7] Interview by Michel Peyrard, "On the Chechnya Front We Realized That Our Leaders Were Mad," *Paris Match*, February 9, 1995, pp. 58–59.

In early April 1995, Lebed revealed his political hand by accepting an invitation to become vice chairman of the Congress of Russian Communities (*Kongress Russkikh obshchin,* or KRO in its Russian acronym), a centrist and moderate nationalist political party formed by Yury Skokov. Lebed described that move as "the beginning of a political battle" in connection with the upcoming December parliamentary election.[8] It was also, not surprisingly in hindsight, the beginning of the end of Grachev's tolerance of Lebed's independent behavior—and thus of Lebed's military career.

Skokov, himself a furtive figure in Yeltsin's inner circle until his own bid for power, had been selected to be the first head of the newly constituted Russian Security Council in July 1992. With little background in security affairs, Skokov was empowered to lead the drafting of a document elaborating a security concept for Russia. That document, allegedly created "in a situation of utter secrecy," was said to be aimed at "counteracting attempts by the United States to achieve unilaterally advantageous conditions in any region of the world." It maintained that Russia "must appear as a force counteracting the United States," which assertedly harbored pretensions of being "the sole leader on the world arena."[9]

Even before his involvement with KRO, Lebed had fallen sufficiently low in his relationship with Grachev that it was clear that the latter and others in his coterie were looking for any excuse to run Lebed out of service. After a steadily escalating estrangement through the spring of 1995, the Ministry of Defense finally moved to resolve its Lebed problem by reorganizing his job out of existence. As a ministry spokesman put it, Grachev had decided to "reform the staff" of Lebed's 14th Army because the latter's manning level was "verging on that of a reduced-strength division" as a result of budget cuts, whereas its headquarters staff of 200 officers had remained un-

---

[8]Interfax, Moscow, April 11, 1995.

[9]Ironically, this manifesto was written at the same time Yeltsin was preparing to go to Washington to firm up the ultimately stillborn Russian-American strategic partnership. It was never adopted by the Security Council. A respected Moscow daily paper flatly branded Skokov a militarist and suggested that Yeltsin had either killed or shelved the document as impolitic "until better times." S. Parkhomenko, "A Certain Skokov: Is a Militaristic Philosophy Again Winning the Russian Administration?" *Nezavisimaia gazeta,* July 31, 1992.

changed. Later, Grachev dissembled that the 14th Army was being reduced in status to an operational group "not out of the caprice of any individual," but because its diminished strength purportedly made it impossible to maintain its "inflated staff."

In a lame attempt at proffering a consolation prize, Grachev offered Lebed the position of deputy commander for training in the Transbaikal Military District, no doubt a barely disguised ploy to get Lebed as far away from Moscow as possible. Predictably, Lebed declined the offer. He also refused an assignment to the General Staff Academy, a job in the Inspectorate, and "other positions" offered by Grachev and by the commander in chief of the Ground Forces, Colonel General Semenov.

With regard to Lebed's political posturing and establishment of a relationship with KRO, Grachev observed that these developments had not gone unnoticed and that Lebed had been "asked to abandon this activity, but he has not yet heeded our suggestion." He added a gratuitous slap by opining that he did not believe that "A. Lebed will make for a strong politician."[10] On a separate occasion, he portrayed Lebed as the army's *enfant terrible* and shrugged off the latter's refusal to accept other posts with a condescending aside that it was evidently "easier to be a populist than to command troops."[11]

In effect, Lebed was being hounded out of service by Grachev for his defiance. With the handwriting on the wall, he tendered his resignation in June 1995, ostensibly in protest over Grachev's contrived decision to downsize his 14th Army. He said that he had thrown in the towel out of exasperation over his continued unsuccessful efforts to change things from below. He finally decided that such efforts were a waste of time: "To achieve anything, you have to act from the top."

---

[10]Quoted in Vladimir Guliyev, "So Far the Swan Song Has Not Become a Hawkish Squawk," *Rossiiskiye vesti*, April 28, 1995. The title is a play on Lebed's last name, which in Russian means "swan," as noted earlier. Lebed's former patron in Afghanistan, General Gromov, remarked more charitably of his former protégé that Lebed has "very many good and bright ideas" and that "his thinking and his view of situations is original," but that he could "nonetheless benefit from a bit more experience both at work and in life." Interview on Moscow Ostankino Television First Channel Network, March 21, 1995.

[11]Interfax, Moscow, May 6, 1995.

Lebed's resignation was accepted by Yeltsin on June 14 with more than a grain of reluctance, since it meant that Lebed was now free to become a challenger to Yeltsin's claim on the presidency. Oleg Lobov, Skokov's successor as Security Council head, offered Lebed a post in the Border Guards. Lebed declined that invitation as well, his eyes now increasingly fixed on a new future in politics. In a parting shot at those in the defense ministry who had conspired to do him in, he warned that his successor in Moldova, Major General Valery Yevnevich, would be "met by pitchforks" by the 14th Army and the local Russian population upon his arrival.[12] Sure enough, when Yevnevich's aircraft approached Tiraspol, 500 women from the surrounding Russian community lay down on the runway to prevent him from landing.

ON THE CAMPAIGN TRAIL

During the early phase of his transition to populism, Lebed was noncommittal on his aspirations to higher office. In July 1994, he stated that he harbored no desire to become president. Even the following year, in the same month he joined up with Skokov, he responded to a query about whether he intended to seek the presidency by declaring that he had "not heard a more idiotic question for a long time."[13] As the final days of his military career neared, however, there was little doubt about Lebed's ambitions. Once his transition was complete, *The Times* of London announced his arrival on the scene as a full-fledged politician with a flourish, stating that having "swapped his fatigues for a double-breasted pinstripe suit and his headquarters for a central Moscow office, the general is presenting himself as an honest, straight-talking patriot untainted by the corruption of his political rivals."[14]

---

[12]The first thing Yevnevich reportedly did was to impose a ban on any 14th Army contacts with the press, which Lebed had allowed to flourish. As part of a defense ministry settling of scores with Lebed after his departure, transfer lists for his subordinates were also drawn up, even though the 14th Army was widely recognized, despite the friction between Lebed and Grachev, as one of the most combat-capable in the Russian military. Rodion Morozov, "The Minister Doesn't Need a Combat-Ready Army," *Obshchaia gazeta*, No. 28, July 13–19, 1995, p. 2.

[13]Interview by Vladimir Kuzmenkin, "The General Who Doesn't Try to Please Anyone," *Vecherniy Novosibirsk*, April 13, 1995.

[14]Interview by Richard Beeston, *The Times* (London), September 27, 1995.

A poll taken in Moscow by the Public Opinion Foundation in late October 1995 found Lebed's popularity rating up from 23 percent the previous month to 32 percent, compared with Zyuganov's at 23 percent, Grigory Yavlinsky's at 22 percent, and Prime Minister Viktor Chernomyrdin's at 21 percent. In the same poll, Zhirinovsky's rating was down to 10 percent.[15] Lebed went into the December parliamentary elections with high confidence, stating that the polls indicated that KRO would get 15 percent of the vote.[16] As a fail-safe option, Lebed also ran independently as a favorite-son candidate from Tula, where he had formerly commanded an airborne division for three years and gained a local following. He artfully dodged a question about whether he had picked that fallback option because he lacked confidence in KRO.[17]

In the end, Lebed won the seat from Tula handily, receiving twice as many votes as his two opponents, one of whom was the mayor of Tula.[18] In light of KRO's failure to score as expected, however, the London *Economist* suggested that Lebed had squandered his appeal as an incorruptible leader by agreeing to subordinate himself to the shadowy and uncharismatic Skokov. That same account further argued that Lebed's "bamboozling" by Skokov raised serious questions about his political judgment.[19]

Such skepticism was echoed two months later by the respected Moscow daily newspaper *Segodnya*, which observed that a recap of Lebed's fleeting career as a would-be politician would easily attest that "all the actions of the former commander of the 14th Army have been either illogical or bound to fail." The author of this critique suggested that in the space of just ten months, Lebed had fallen "from a promising politician, believed to be the most probable contestant for the presidency, into an ordinary deputy, being at best among the top ten aspirants for the Kremlin." He added that Lebed

---

[15]Interfax, Moscow, October 30, 1995.

[16]Interview by Fiametta Cucurnia, "Lebed Approaches the Kremlin: I Will Save Russia," *La Repubblica* (Rome), November 12, 1995.

[17]Interview with Rodion Morozov, "Lebed Talks Without Skokov's Approval," *Obshchaia gazeta*, No. 47, November 23–29, 1995, p. 9.

[18]ITAR-TASS, Moscow, December 18, 1995.

[19]*The Economist* (London), December 23, 1995, p. 61.

appeared to be "at a loss" ever since he was undercut by his duplicitous sponsor Skokov, and that he obviously had failed to grasp the fact that there is a difference between a popularity rating and the actual sentiments of voters. He compared Lebed unfavorably with Aleksandr Rutskoi, another ambitious military hero who had launched into an abortive career in politics five years earlier with "virtually no appropriate skills and experience."[20]

One insightful Russian analysis suggested that the single biggest weakness of KRO was the rivalry between Lebed and Skokov. That assessment drew a comparison between KRO and the similarly riven Democratic Russia movement, noting that "like-minded individuals in a struggle for power, upon coming to power, immediately begin to split into factions." Lebed enjoyed the popularity, while Skokov, albeit KRO's head, was not considered a strong figure. The analysis suggested, dead on target in retrospect, that Lebed's coattails might not suffice to carry other KRO candidates into the Duma.[21]

Three weeks before the parliamentary election, there had been rumors in Moscow of a falling out between Lebed and Skokov. Skokov gave a major campaign speech on behalf of KRO in which he did not even mention Lebed's name.[22] The conflict between the two reportedly reached a point where Skokov allegedly banned Lebed from giving interviews without his permission—a sanction that even Grachev had not been able to enforce while Lebed was 14th Army commander.

The London *Economist* later declared that Lebed's presidential prospects had collapsed because KRO did so poorly in the parliamentary campaign.[23] That, viewed in retrospect, was clearly a pre-

---

[20]Gleb Cherkasov, "Aleksandr Lebed Has Set Out to Sea All Alone. The Future of His Political Career Will Be Decided in the Next Few Months," *Segodnya*, March 7, 1996. This article went on to note that Lebed's political future would be determined by the manner in which he conducted his election campaign. It added, presciently in hindsight, that Lebed need not win the presidential race to remain a credible political force.

[21]"New Favorite or Nine-Day Wonder? The Congress of Russian Communities on the Eve of the Parliamentary Elections," *Rossiiskiye vesti*, November 14, 1995.

[22]Speech by Yury Skokov at the Fifth Congress of the Russian Congress of Communities, "A State for the People," *Zavtra*, No. 47, November 1995, pp. 1–3.

[23]"The Sphinx in the Kremlin," *The Economist* (London), January 6, 1996, p. 37.

mature rush to judgment. On December 28, Lebed announced his intent to run for president, becoming the first contestant formally to throw his hat into the ring. He further suggested that he might campaign "in agreement" with the communists, although that idea later proved to be a nonstarter.[24]

Many analysts in Moscow speculated that KRO performed so poorly in the December election because Skokov had made the tactical error of keeping Lebed on a short leash. They suggested that Lebed might fare better in the future under his own agenda. Certainly the pre-election polls showed strong support for Lebed's declared goal of bringing order to Russia's chaos. Before the election, he had always received the highest ratings of any politician mentioned as a possible successor to Yeltsin.

Once safely ensconced in the Duma, Lebed cut his ties with KRO and pursued his quest for the presidency as an independent.[25] He was sharply critical of KRO for the drag that it had imposed on his earlier effort to enter the political arena. He acknowledged KRO's later offer to assist in his presidential campaign with, at best, a backhanded note of gratitude: "They support me. Well, thanks. But I can't consider myself bound by any obligation. They have good people in the provinces. I can work with them. But I'm not going to let them be a millstone around my neck a second time."[26]

Lebed was rumored early on to have been offered the post of defense minister by Yeltsin. Indeed, there were suggestions that Lebed might be invited by Yeltsin to replace Grachev *before* the June election in an attempt by the president to kill two birds with one stone by unburdening himself of his tarnished defense minister in favor of one who commanded unqualified respect throughout the ranks, while at the

---

[24]Carol J. Williams, "Charismatic Ex-General to Run for Russian Presidency," *Los Angeles Times*, December 29, 1995, and Michael Specter, "Army Hero Enters Russian Race, Posing a Big Threat to Reformers," *New York Times*, December 29, 1995.

[25]KRO finally dropped Skokov as its titular leader at its congress on May 29, 1996.

[26]"General Lebed: 'Maybe I Should Accept Minister of Culture?!'" *Komsomolskaia pravda*, May 30, 1996. One Moscow commentator shrewdly remarked that Lebed owed part of his success to the fact that "the team this time did not include the deadly ally, Yury Skokov, who is worth a dozen enemies." Feliks Babitskii, "A Predictable Concession," *Rossiiskiye vesti*, June 19, 1996.

same time eliminating Lebed as a threat to his own position.[27] The Moscow rumor mill had been busy with speculation that Yeltsin was nearing a decision to pin the blame for the war in Chechnya on Grachev and move him to a less visible post as a campaign concession to his critics.[28]

The problem with that scenario was that Lebed would have been as untamed as Yeltsin's defense minister as he was as Grachev's 14th Army commander in Moldova. He would have felt no obligation whatever to give Yeltsin the loyalty that the latter had successfully commanded from Grachev. Maintaining that he was "not a puppet," Lebed declared that he would not accept such an appointment in any case. He indicated that some 90 percent of the defense ministry's structure would have to be cleaned out before he would even consider taking on that position.[29]

In the end, by now with more ambitious goals in mind, Lebed ruled out settling for any such second-order option. He stated that "various candidates" had offered him a role in their shadow cabinets, but that he was not interested, since he is "a soldier, not a chastizer."[30] He later expanded on this, stating that "the defense minister should be a professional, a respected general. They simply don't understand that—they give it to their Grachevs. . . . I have a good name. To receive a ministerial portfolio on the basis of purely political games is to lose your good name, to cover it in mud. . . . The mili-

---

[27]Aleksandr Sveshnikov, "Where Are the Rooks to Spend the Winter? Feed for the Swan Has Already Been Provided," *Moskovskii komsomolets*, November 14, 1995. The title is a play on Grachev's surname, which means "rook" in Russian, and on Lebed's, which means "swan," as noted earlier.

[28]One such rumored possibility was that Yeltsin might move Grachev to take over the reins of the Security Council from its existing head, Oleg Lobov, who at the time was recovering from heart surgery. To this suggestion, one anonymous senior Security Council staffer retorted angrily that Grachev "is not suited to the tasks of providing analytical support for the activity of the head of state, which is what the efforts of the Security Council's interagency commissions are directed toward." Dispatch by Tamara Zamyatina, ITAR-TASS, Moscow, March 11, 1996.

[29]Interview by Juan Cicero, "It Looks Like Yeltsin's Time Has Come Sooner or Later," *ABC* (Madrid), October 29, 1995.

[30]Tatyana Selivanova, ITAR-TASS dispatch, Moscow, May 7, 1996.

tary won't forgive that. I wouldn't forgive myself. The army won't accept a minister who won his post in the political casino."[31]

A high-level aide to Colonel General Mikhail Kolesnikov, the chief of the General Staff, however, told a foreign reporter that Lebed had indeed been offered the defense ministry by Yeltsin and had been given until May 15 to decide. By that same account, Lebed also was given assurances from Yeltsin that some fifteen corrupt generals in Grachev's inner circle would be removed. The anonymous source speculated that Lebed would eventually strike a bargain with Yeltsin, so long as the former's path "was cleared by means of a prior sweep" and that Lebed would be permitted by Yeltsin to appoint his own people to subordinate positions.[32] (The eventual announcement of Colonel General Igor Rodionov's selection to be Grachev's successor on July 17, discussed in greater detail below, went a long way toward confirming the broad validity of that account.)[33]

Once his campaign hit its stride, Lebed hired some high-powered media consultants to help soften his image and to develop a barrage of appealing television commercials depicting him as a devoted crime-fighter and opponent of corruption.[34] He later had a 27-minute audience with Yeltsin in the Kremlin on May 2 at the latter's invitation, in the first such tete-à-tete between the Russian president and any of his political rivals. It was not revealed what was said or

---

[31] *Komsomolskaia pravda,* May 30, 1996. At about that same time, an unattributed document that included Lebed among fifteen candidates said to be under consideration by Yeltsin to replace Grachev was making the rounds in Moscow. The document indicated that negotiations were under way to offer Lebed the position of defense minister "in exchange for his withdrawal from the electoral campaign." Interestingly, the document also indicated that Colonel General Igor Rodionov, who ultimately got the job, was "no longer being considered at the present time." See "Supplemental List of Persons Viewed as Candidates for Appointment to the Office of Minister of Defense, Decision on Which Has Been Postponed," *Moskovskiye novosti,* No. 21, May 26–June 2, 1996, p. 10.

[32] Giuletto Chiesa, "Deep Throat at Staff Headquarters," *La Stampa* (Turin), May 10, 1996.

[33] After the announcement of Rodionov's appointment, the daily Moscow newspaper *Izvestiia* pointed out that the month-long delay in filling the post of defense minister left vacant by Grachev's dismissal was the longest pause since 1802. Cited by ITAR-TASS, July 17, 1996.

[34] Michael R. Gordon, "From War Hero to Populist Politician," *New York Times,* June 18, 1996.

what deals may have been struck, although there was speculation afterward that Yeltsin had offered Lebed an important post in exchange for the latter's dropping out of the race, a supposition immediately denied by Lebed's campaign headquarters.[35]

Yeltsin provided financial support to Lebed's campaign during the final week to draw votes from Zyuganov. He also offered Lebed extensive television coverage and his own personal attention.[36] A Lebed confidant, Dmitri Rogozin, said that Lebed had been in secret negotiations with Yeltsin for months before the election and, as early as January, was drawing financial and organizational aid from Gennady Burbulis, one of Yeltsin's closest political strategists. According to Rogozin, tacit "protocols" and "understandings" were arrived at, although nothing was formally committed to paper. The main understanding between the two contenders was that the communists were the common enemy. There was also a tacit understanding that Yeltsin and Lebed would not attack one another. Lebed reportedly had indicated that he wanted to be named vice president, yet he understood that any such concession by Yeltsin would require an amendment to the constitution, which would be slow and problematic. By Rogozin's account, Lebed further insisted on Grachev's prompt removal as a precondition for his joining the Yeltsin camp.[37]

As expected, Lebed failed to reach an accord with Yavlinsky and Fyodorov in their fateful meeting on May 15.[38] Lebed later stressed that he would join the so-called "Third Force" only if he were to be designated its presidential candidate.[39] He said that his inability to strike a bargain offered in the end a "good reflection of the situation" and that any such agreement would have yielded an unnatural relationship in any case: "I said long ago that a three-headed alliance is a

---

[35]"Segodnya" newscast, Moscow NTV, May 2, 1996.

[36]See William Safire, "Round 1: Yeltsin," *New York Times*, June 17, 1996.

[37]John Helmer, "Inside Kremlin Purge—Lebed-Yeltsin Alliance Falters," *The Journal of Commerce*, no date given.

[38]"Segodnya" newscast, Moscow NTV, May 3, 1996.

[39]Dispatch by Viktor Yelmakov, ITAR-TASS World Service, Moscow, May 15, 1996. Lebed added that he saw Yavlinskii as a "splendid candidate" for prime minister and offered to establish a special post for Fyodorov as vice president.

fire-breathing dragon, an interesting monster yet helpless at our latitudes. Yavlinsky is conducting negotiations with the president, and I learn about them from television."[40]

On election eve, the popular General Boris Gromov was touted by some as the most likely candidate to replace Grachev as defense minister. Gromov was said to want the post, although knowledgeable observers suggested that his politicking for the job might well prevent him from getting it.[41] Earlier, Gromov had been a harsh critic of nearly all aspects of Yeltsin's leadership. Moscow speculation also saw the post going possibly to Andrei Kokoshin, General Kolesnikov, or General Andrei Nikolayev.[42]

As election day neared, Yeltsin lost no time offering symbolic gestures aimed at attracting votes from his detractors and other fence-sitters undecided about him but less enthusiastic over the prospect of a return to power of the communists. After many promises, he finally acceded to a ceasefire agreement with the Chechen resistance on May 27, with the cessation of hostilities scheduled to go into effect at midnight on June 1.[43] (That agreement quickly proved to be short-lived. As discussed in Chapter Nine, subsequent fighting in Chechnya has been as intense as ever.) Four days before the election, Yeltsin also promoted each of his service chiefs to four-star rank in a transparent bid for their support.[44]

In what the *Wall Street Journal* later acknowledged to have been a "well-run" campaign, Lebed focused in the end on the single hot-button issue of crime and corruption.[45] To everyone's surprise, he finished in a remarkably strong third place in the 10-man race, gaining more than eleven million votes in an election that saw a 70-percent voter turnout. Polls conducted only a week earlier had indi-

---

[40]Personal interview, "Aleksandr Lebed: My Program Has to Be Explained to Everyone," *Sovetskaia molodezh*, May 21, 1996.

[41]Anatoly Veslo, "Boris Gromov Has Become Boris Yeltsin's Proxy. The Popular General Has Changed His Orientation," *Segodnya*, May 14, 1996.

[42]See "Storming the Military's Olympus," *Moskovskiye novosti*, May 26–June 2, 1996.

[43]Neela Banerjee and Steve Liesman, "Russia, Chechnya Agree to Cease-Fire," *Wall Street Journal*, May 28, 1996.

[44]Dispatch by Anatoly Yurkin, ITAR-TASS, Moscow, June 13, 1996.

[45]"It's Up to Yeltsin," *Wall Street Journal*, June 18, 1996.

cated that Lebed would win no more than 7 percent, although that figure grew to 11 percent just before the election.[46] Exit polls indicated that 47 percent of voters in the military had supported Lebed, with the airborne troops backing him almost unanimously.[47]

Even before the dust had settled, and now well mindful of the new power his third-place win had conferred on him, Lebed declared that he needed "a position with decisionmaking authority" and one in which he could "organize the fight against crime and prevent extremists from both the right and left from plunging the country into an abyss of bloody chaos."[48] A parliamentary deputy close to Yeltsin, Aleksandr Shokhin, concurrently told journalists that the president might create for Lebed a post that combined the roles of national security adviser and deputy prime minister in charge of police, defense, and security forces.

Zyuganov also courted Lebed, publicly offering on one occasion to make the former general his prime minister. After later losing in the July runoff, Zyuganov turned on Lebed, proclaiming that the latter had sold out to Yeltsin and could expect the same fate that had earlier befallen Rutskoi. Zyuganov sourly added that the Yeltsinites "are more in need of Lebed's votes than they are of an effective fight against crime."[49] His reference to Rutskoi was a less than apt comparison. A major difference between Lebed and Rutskoi, said a former Lebed colleague, Colonel Viktor Baranets, is that "Rutskoi did not have the armed forces or 11 million voters behind him. If Yeltsin thinks he can exploit Lebed and then drop him, he should think twice."[50]

The day after the election, Lebed told Radio Liberty that he was not interested in the defense minister portfolio and that he would not accept the post of Security Council secretary either, brushing the latter

---

[46]Carol J. Williams, "Yeltsin Edging Out Communist, But a Runoff Looms," *Los Angeles Times*, June 17, 1996.

[47]Denis Baranets, "To the Polling Station, Forward March," *Moskovskiye novosti*, June 16-23, 1996.

[48]Quoted in Carol J. Williams, "Close First Vote Seen as Helping Yeltsin in Runoff," *Los Angeles Times*, June 17, 1996.

[49]"Vesti" newscast, Russian Television Network, Moscow, June 18, 1996.

[50]Quoted in Bruce W. Nelan, "Rise of the General," *Time*, July 1, 1996, p. 44.

aside as a "functionary's job."[51] By repeatedly stressing his special interest in fighting crime and corruption, he hinted that he might be angling to head the Ministry of Internal Affairs, although he gave no overt indication of that.

AS YELTSIN APPOINTEE AND WOULD-BE HEIR APPARENT

With his victory in the first round of the election safely behind him and his position as a presidential finalist thus assured, there was instant speculation both in Moscow and in the West that Yeltsin, mindful of Lebed's sudden empowerment as a potential kingmaker, would seek every opportunity to enlist the latter's support. Sure enough, the Russian president "hit a political gusher," as the *New York Times* put it, by coopting Lebed as his security adviser and secretary of the Security Council the very first day after the election.[52] This coup de main had the effect of helping to protect Yeltsin against charges of being a party to corruption and cronyism, while at the same time conferring on Lebed real political clout for the first time, plus creating a springboard from which to nurture his own presidential ambitions.

That same day, Yeltsin signed a decree expanding the powers of the Security Council secretary to include overseeing military reform and orchestrating the fight against crime and corruption through the joint efforts of the defense and interior ministries, the Federal Security Service (FSB), and the Foreign Intelligence Service.[53] A week later, on June 25, Lebed was tapped by Yeltsin to chair a commission on the vetting of military and other senior security-related personnel appointments.[54]

At his first post-election news conference, on June 18, with Lebed at his side, Yeltsin coyly touted Lebed as his designated successor, in an

---

[51]Alessandra Stanley, "Yeltsin Courting Losing Candidates in Russian Voting," *New York Times*, June 18, 1996.

[52]"The Yeltsin-Lebed Alliance," *New York Times*, June 19, 1996.   In the latter assignment, Lebed replaced Oleg Lobov, who was moved upstairs to become deputy prime minister.

[53]Interfax, Moscow, June 18, 1996.

[54]Dispatch by Andrei Shtorkh, ITAR-TASS World Service, Moscow, June 25, 1996.

obvious appeal to the latter's electoral constituency. In response to a reporter's leading question as to whether the president regarded Lebed as his heir apparent, Yeltsin replied: "It's too early to speak about that." Then, all but winking, he added: "You are thinking correctly, however."[55] Said Yeltsin of his new compact with Lebed: "This is not just an appointment, this is a union of two politicians. This is a union of two programs." In effect, Yeltsin said that he had embraced Lebed's platform and agenda as his own: "I think those who voted for Aleksandr Ivanovich sent a message to the president to implement the good things they saw in [Lebed's] program. . . . Therefore, I must somewhat adjust my own program accordingly and include in it such issues as military reform, security issues, the fight against crime and corruption."

Lebed's rise to an insider role in the Yeltsin government prompted jaundiced reactions from some reformist quarters. Yeltsin's former human rights adviser, Sergei Kovalyov, for example, warned that the president's cooptation of Lebed inevitably foreshadowed "a greater tendency by the authorities to act in undemocratic ways."[56] This respected democrat, who had had an earlier falling out with Yeltsin over the latter's initiation of the war in Chechnya, later noted that "the duo of Yeltsin and Lebed is dangerous" and will occasion an increase in state "control over society" and "nontransparency in politics."[57]

For his part, Lebed said that his main concern in signing on with Yeltsin was to prevent an explosion of unrest in Russia. He commented that he saw the likelihood as high as 70 percent that a civil war could break out in the aftermath of the election.[58] He once declared that he would withdraw from the presidential race only if he were offered firm and serious guarantees of a position that would help him prevent this, adding, somewhat disingenuously, "I don't

---

[55]ITAR-TASS, Moscow, June 18, 1996.

[56]Quoted in Lee Hockstader, "Lebed's Meteoric Ascent," *Washington Post,* June 25, 1996.

[57]Quoted in Michael Specter, "Yeltsin's Moment: Can the President Build on His Victory?" *New York Times,* July 5, 1996.

[58]Information Agency *Ekho Moskvy,* May 13, 1996.

care about power. I just want to prevent a war in the country. I can feel a civil war in my bones."[59]

Exit polls indicated that 44 percent of those who voted for Lebed had affirmed that they would support Yeltsin in the runoff. The final tally came closer to 54 percent.[60] According to the generally reliable All-Russia Center for the Study of Public Opinion, or VTsIOM in its Russian acronym, most of Lebed's supporters in the June 16 election were middle-aged men with high-school educations, their numbers spread equally among cities, towns, and villages.[61] The former head of Yeltsin's analytical center, Mark Urnov, later admitted that he "could not be sure" what percentage of Yeltsin's 14-point lead in the July 3 runoff was attributable to voters who had cast ballots for Lebed and Yavlinsky in the first round. "We won't be able to distinguish this clearly," Urnov said.[62]

The announcement of Lebed's appointment as security adviser, along with his consent in principle to join the Yeltsin camp, prompted immediate speculation that Yeltsin was interested in Lebed to cash in on the latter's appeal in order to ensure his own re-election rather than to groom Lebed to be his successor. Later, however, when asked before the runoff what guarantees he could offer that he would not discard Lebed after the final results were in, the president replied that he had never traded in government posts and that his signature on the decree appointing Lebed was not the only one: "I think the signatures of the millions of voters who cast their ballots for him on June 16 stand next to it as well. Their trust can't be

---

[59]Interfax, Moscow, May 8, 1996.

[60]Exit polls conducted for the *New York Times* reportedly indicated that the "overwhelming majority" of the 15 million who supported Lebed in the first round voted for Yeltsin in the runoff. Cited in Michael Specter, "Yeltsin Defeats Communist Foe By a Surprisingly Wide Margin; Health Issue Looms for 2nd Term," *New York Times*, July 4, 1996.

[61]Yury Levada, "Three-Fourths of the Electorate Intend to Vote," *Izvestiia*, June 25, 1996.

[62]Quoted in John Helmer, "Yeltsin Victory a 'Tight Box,'" *The Straits Times*, Singapore, July 5, 1996. In fact, according to a detailed polling analysis done at Harvard University's Russian Research Center, Yeltsin's cooptation of Lebed, in the end, did little to affect Yeltsin's performance in the July 3 runoff election. Before Yeltsin brought Lebed aboard, 53 percent of the electorate planned to vote for him in the second round, just 0.7 percent fewer than actually did so on July 3. See Daniel Treisman, "Why Yeltsin Won," *Foreign Affairs*, September/October 1996, p. 65.

ignored. I'm sure Aleksandr Lebed has come to work earnestly and for the long haul. He is a person who can beat crime and restore order."[63]

At the same press conference at which he unveiled the selection of Lebed as his new security adviser, Yeltsin announced, as "another piece of news," that General Grachev had been relieved of his position as defense minister.[64] As recently as late May, just two weeks before the election, Yeltsin had given Grachev at least lip-service support, saying that "overall, I am satisfied with the work of top ministry officials and the defense minister."[65] However, once he saw that he had a clear shot at the brass ring on July 3, Yeltsin no longer had any need to retain Grachev.

The timing of Yeltsin's dismissal of Grachev was exquisite. Just two weeks before, an "informed source" in Moscow speculated that the president would not relieve his unpopular but loyal minister before the June 16 election.[66] As it turned out, his sacking of Grachev immediately after the first round of the election, with the runoff against Zyuganov still looming ahead, helped to underwrite Yeltsin's claim to being a backer of serious military reform. It also strengthened the credibility of his call for the votes of Lebed's supporters.

Lebed claimed personal credit for the removal of Grachev. It was Yeltsin, however, who summoned Grachev and apprised the latter of his plans to bring in Lebed. In response, Grachev reportedly stated his refusal on principle to work under his former subordinate and penned a letter of resignation on the spot. No doubt Grachev's dismissal was a precondition levied by Lebed for signing on with Yeltsin, although it was the president himself who delivered the message to his discredited but long-loyal defense leader. The chief of the General Staff, General Kolesnikov, was appointed acting defense

---

[63]Interfax, Moscow, June 30, 1996.

[64]"Vesti" newscast, Russian Television Network, Moscow, June 18, 1996.

[65]Dispatch by Anatoly Yurkin, ITAR-TASS World Service, Moscow, May 29, 1996. See also Michael Gordon, "Yeltsin Moves To Win Favor In His Military," *New York Times*, June 15, 1996. This account presciently observed that "so strong is support for Mr. Lebed in the military that the general's ultimate decision to endorse or rebuff Mr. Yeltsin, if the election goes to a runoff as expected, could prove decisive."

[66]Dispatch by Artyom Protasenko, ITAR-TASS, Moscow, May 28, 1996.

minister. Grachev's future prospects remain unclear and, in all likelihood, are yet to be determined. There was early speculation that he might be offered the post of commander in chief of the Joint Armed Forces of the Commonwealth of Independent States. An alternative possibility mentioned was that he would be named Russia's representative to NATO.[67]

Lebed also had a hand in the firing of seven generals who were alleged to be cronies of Grachev. These included the chief of the Main Operations Directorate of the General Staff, Colonel General Viktor Barynkin; another department chief, Colonel General Anatoly Sitnov; the head of the international military cooperation department, Colonel General Dmitri Kharchenko; and Grachev's executive officer, Colonel General Valery Lapshov.[68] (Interestingly, Lieutenant General Gennady Ivanov, Grachev's principal deputy for military reform, seems to have survived this initial housecleaning.[69]) As Lebed explained after the dismissals were announced, these individuals, along with Grachev's press secretary, Yelena Agapova, had allegedly gathered in a defense ministry meeting room to devise a plan to elicit grassroots support for Grachev's reinstatement among commanding generals in the Moscow Military District and elsewhere. In preempting this attempted gambit, Lebed said that he had directed the defense ministry's command post not to forward any messages from these schemers to the field. He also said that he had instructed all generals in the surrounding area not to send messages of condolence

---

[67]See Andrei Poleshchuk, "A 'New Broom' in the President's Hands," *Nezavisimaia gazeta*, June 19, 1996.

[68]David Hoffman, "Yeltsin Gives Campaign Rival Wide Power as Security Czar," *Washington Post*, June 19, 1996.

[69]One hostile reporter commented that people in the defense ministry are now asking why General Ivanov, "one of Grachev's closest comrades in arms and his adviser on military policy and reform, who has seemingly made a mess of everything he could make a mess of, has survived." This reporter charged that, at just the right moment, Ivanov, who "possessed all the information," sided with Lebed and rushed to the embrace of Lebed's subordinate, Colonel Denisov, who had been Lebed's secret eyes and ears in the Grachev defense ministry. As a result, Denisov allegedly became deputy secretary of the Security Council and Ivanov became Lebed's campaign coordinator at the Ministry of Defense. "It is all so cozy that it makes you sick." Igor Chernyak, "Generals Will Be Fired in Platoons," *Komsomolskaia pravda*, July 2, 1996. It bears noting here that General Ivanov has been a centrally important figure in sustaining the Russian-American military-to-military contact relationship.

to Grachev and that any who did would be personally charged for the cable.

Lebed moved promptly to quash rumors that these allies of Grachev's had been plotting a mini-coup, saying that what they were up to was "not an attempted coup" but "an attempt to pressure the president" by rallying the troops to lobby for Grachev's reinstatement. The dispatch with which these dismissals were carried out suggests that they were preplanned by Lebed, presumably with Yeltsin's prior consent.

The dismissal of Grachev naturally prompted immediate speculation as to who might be named his successor. With Lebed now in the catbird seat as Yeltsin's Security Council secretary and with his sights on loftier goals, the former general was well beyond being a contender by that time, even though he might have settled for the job earlier under the right conditions. Surprisingly, Lebed had unkind words for one putative candidate who had once been high on his list, General Boris Gromov. When asked for his opinion of Gromov, Lebed replied: "What do I think of General Gromov? On second thought, I do not think of General Gromov. He was once a very good general who shortchanged himself."[70] Elsewhere, Lebed said that "Gromov used to be a good general who later dissipated his energy on minor things."[71] Perhaps his awareness of Gromov's desire for the job, Gromov's past role as Lebed's commanding officer in Afghanistan, and the fact that he had spoken patronizingly about Lebed during the early days of the latter's evolution as a populist all added up to a conclusion on Lebed's part that Gromov would simply be too much for him to handle as defense minister.

Only days later, Yeltsin further announced the dismissals of three of his most intimate confidants—his personal security chief and right-hand man, Aleksandr Korzhakov; the head of the Federal Security Service, Mikhail Barsukov; and First Deputy Prime Minister Oleg Soskovets. This summary sacking of three of the president's closest and, by some accounts, most corrupt cronies amounted to a tectonic shift in Kremlin politics and significantly affected Lebed's political

---

[70]"Vesti" newscast, Russian Television Network, Moscow, June 18, 1996.

[71]Information Agency *Ekho Moskvy*, Moscow, June 18, 1996.

standing. There was an early rush among some reporters to view it as yet another testament to Lebed's new-found leverage in Moscow's inner decisionmaking circles. As one impressed American correspondent, implying as much, said of that episode in the immediate wake of Grachev's firing: "Not bad for five days' work."[72]

The best guess, however, is that the easing out of these three Yeltsin principals was not a Lebed-inspired act so much as the doing of Yeltsin's newly appointed chief of staff, Anatoly Chubais, who managed to prevail over the so-called "party of war" in an unexpected test of strength.[73] The contretemps began when two Yeltsin campaign staffers, Arkady Yevstafiev and Sergei Lisovskii, were detained at the White House for allegedly leaving, without written authorization, with a box containing some $500,000 in cash. Planting money is an old KGB trick, and this may well have been a staged provocation. Whatever it was, the event galvanized Chubais into prompt counteraction and set off a long night of Kremlin infighting. Commenting later on Lebed's televised demand for an explanation of the detentions once the smoke had cleared, Chubais said that the new security adviser's firm stand "worked like a cold shower on hot heads."[74] According to one opinion poll in Moscow, six of ten respondents approved of Yeltsin's action.[75]

Lebed insisted afterward that he personally had no hand in the firing of Korzhakov or Soskovets, and that he had made no overt efforts toward that end: "I guess the president had been thinking about these dismissals for a long time." Lebed added that his ascension to Yeltsin's entourage had been only a "catalyst of the process. . . . I neither appointed nor dismissed them. It's the president's business."[76]

---

[72]Jonas Bernstein, "Lebed's Way," *The American Spectator*, August 1996, p. 57.

[73]Although they were later to encounter their own differences, Chubais was reported at the outset to have Lebed's solid support in this move. Afterward, Chubais declared that the showdown with the trio was the culmination of "a long and arduous struggle." Quoted in Michael R. Gordon, "A Onetime Scapegoat Savors Taste of Revenge," *New York Times*, June 21, 1996. See also Alessandra Stanley, "Election Looming, Yeltsin Dismisses Three Top Hard-Liners," *New York Times*, June 21, 1996.

[74]Quoted in Richard Boudreaux, "Yeltsin Fires Three Cabinet Hard-Liners," *Los Angeles Times*, June 21, 1996.

[75]Cited in "Russia's Run-Off Ructions," *The Economist* (London), June 29, 1996, p. 45.

[76]Interfax, Moscow, July 2, 1996.

When asked for his personal opinion of Korzhakov and his dismissal by Yeltsin, Lebed responded elliptically, saying only that Korzhakov "was simply too active a man."[77] Although portrayed by some among Yeltsin's following as a foiled coup, the provocation by Korzhakov and his allies was dismissed by one well-placed observer, Presidential Council member Sergei Karaganov, as "very small, petty, an administrative illegality."[78] Korzhakov may well have sealed his own fate weeks earlier (on May 4) when he suggested that the election should be postponed, to the consternation of Yeltsin, who promptly disavowed the idea.[79]

Lebed's solo performance under the spotlight as Yeltsin's anointed prima donna did not last long. Prime Minister Viktor Chernomyrdin, in particular, had seemed to be doing a slow burn while Lebed was making daily headlines around the world from center stage. No sooner had Yeltsin reappointed Chernomyrdin as prime minister than the latter locked horns with Lebed, with Chernomyrdin defending his turf condescendingly against the upstart interloper. For openers, Chernomyrdin intoned that there was "no direct link" between Lebed's appointment and the dismissal of Grachev, an assertion that was clearly belied by every indication to the contrary. He also said that he had heard nothing about any alleged military plot, and that any and all rumors to that effect were "nonsense."[80] That second statement may have been closer to the mark.

Lebed's broader ambitions were likewise bound to stick in Chernomyrdin's throat. Within days of entering the Kremlin, the new security adviser had reportedly urged Yeltsin yet again to make him vice president, a post that does not exist under the 1993 Russian constitution. Such an appointment would put Lebed in direct line to replace Yeltsin, displacing Chernomyrdin. To this, Chernomyrdin retorted sharply, suggesting that Lebed should "calm down a bit" and

---

[77]Quoted in "To Establish Order," *Der Spiegel* (Hamburg), June 24, 1996, pp. 129–131.

[78]Quoted in Carol J. Williams, "Alleged Coup Plot Points to Russia's Fragile Democracy," *Los Angeles Times*, June 21, 1996.

[79]Korzhakov reportedly said that "a lot of influential people are in favor of postponing the elections, and I'm in favor of it too because we need stability." Quoted in Victoria Clark, "Yeltsin's Man Stills His Master's Voice," *The Observer* (London), May 5, 1996.

[80]Dispatch by Artyom Protasenko, ITAR-TASS, Moscow, June 18, 1996, and Interfax, Moscow, June 18, 1996.

that "I personally do not see any particular need for this post."[81] He further made a disparaging allusion to what Rutskoi had done to discredit it.[82]

Lebed's early advocacy of Colonel General Igor Rodionov, the commandant of the General Staff Academy, as his personal candidate to replace Grachev as defense minister entailed going out on a limb in a major way. An obvious power play, it could have backfired severely had Yeltsin kept his own counsel and chosen someone else. Seen in hindsight, it was a bold gamble on Lebed's part. Lebed clearly spoke prematurely, however, when he stated that Yeltsin would announce the name of his new defense minister on June 24 or 25.[83] That indicated that he still had much to learn about when to speak out and when to remain silent.

Lebed has freely admitted that he is a novice to Moscow dealings and that he is less than comfortable in the political arena. He once commented that as long as he was in the military he felt "like a fish in water." In contrast, he has described politics as "a game without rules."[84] Yet despite this, Lebed has worked hard since the parliamentary election last December to moderate his image and soften its rougher edges. He is the first to concede the shortcomings in his communication skills, having suggested once before the June election that his campaign might have greater effect "if we were able to explain my program to the people. . . . If 7 percent are ready to vote for me today, this means that I succeeded in explaining it to 7 percent; if 10 percent—this mean I succeeded in explaining it to 10 percent. I must continue to explain."[85]

---

[81]Quoted in Lee Hockstader, "Buoyant Yeltsin Retains Premier," *Washington Post,* July 5, 1996.

[82]Lebed had already expressed an equally sharp counter to this viewpoint: "If someone has had bad luck with his wife, it does not mean that the institution of marriage should be abolished." Interview on Russian Public Television First Channel Network, Moscow, July 1, 1996.

[83]"Presidential Bulletin" feature, Interfax, Moscow, June 21, 1996.

[84]Interview by Andrzej Rybak, "The Difference? I Don't Drink!" *Die Woche* (Hamburg), December 1, 1995.

[85]Personal interview, "Aleksandr Lebed: My Program Has to Be Explained to Everyone," *Sovetskaia molodezh*, May 21, 1996.

Consistent with this self-assessment, Lebed has not yet shown a great flair for politics. Nevertheless, he is now a well-positioned insider with a clear mandate to make his influence felt in resolving many problems that have long been of core concern to him. Beyond that, he remains keenly interested in eventually securing Yeltsin's job, and he commands enough credibility as a contender to make it vital that he be taken seriously by the West. As a first step, this means looking beyond the overly impressionistic characterizations of him that have been sketched out above to a more searching review of the evidence bearing on Lebed's substantive views on the issues that matter most.

Chapter Four

ON RUSSIA AND ITS PLACE IN THE WORLD

Lebed lacks an ideological core and is not an imperialist by inclination. He has conceded that it was communism and its corrupt leadership that put Russia in the sad condition it demonstrates today by militarizing society and letting the defense establishment bleed the rest of the economy dry. He has insisted more than once that he is not bent on recovering a lost empire.

That said, Lebed stands squarely in the midst of the Russian nationalist camp. He lacks the shrillness of Zhirinovsky and is the more tempered patriot one would expect a Russian general to be. But he is deeply wedded to the idea of the Russian homeland and displays measured outrage at his country's loss of its former international stature and self-respect. Jacob Kipp has portrayed him as a "populist-nationalist," noting how "in place of S. S. Uvarov's trinity of orthodoxy, autocracy, and nationality from the reign of Nicholas I, Lebed offers his own: orthodoxy, the creative genius of the Russian people, and the valor of the Russian army."[1]

To date, Lebed has not elaborated much on his conception of "whither Russia." He has said more than enough, however, to telegraph at least the essence of his thinking on Russia's character and destiny, on the prospects for a return to former Soviet boundaries, and proper approaches toward dealing with the West.

---

[1]Jacob W. Kipp, "The Political Ballet of General Aleksandr Ivanovich Lebed: Implications for Russia's Presidential Elections," *Problems of Post-Communism*, July–August 1996, p. 43.

LEBED'S VISION OF RUSSIA

The biggest obstacle to Russia's recovery, in Lebed's view, is the country's depleted strength. He once remarked that the one-time superpower "is turning into a sick, skinny elephant upon which all varieties of rats and hyenas have begun feeding."[2] He has also declared that if the problem is not corrected, Russia will soon be reduced to performing three demeaning functions: providing cheap labor, supplying cheap natural resources, and serving as the world's garbage dump.[3]

In Lebed's assessment, the roots of Russia's weakness go back to the earliest days of the Soviet state. Citing the civil war, Stalin's persecutions, World War II, and subsequent mass emigration as the main culprits, he maintains that these ravages severely damaged the country's "genetic pool" and that much more of such stress can cause the country to perish.[4] He has flatly stated that Russia "will not survive a third war in one century."[5]

On the positive side, he has noted that the country has great resiliency and staying power, and he has warned the West not to count Russia out prematurely: "The world has decided that the bear is dead and has sighed with relief. But this is a mistake. Russia occupies an eighth of the world's territory and is inhabited by 150 million very patient people who have in their veins the blood of Suvorov and Zhukov, who knew a thing or two about winning."[6]

Typically, Lebed evades the question of what would constitute the most appropriate strategy for Russia, suggesting once that answering that would take "three days without lunch breaks." He adds that national security strategy "is not something to be discussed in the open press" and that he will speak to it publicly only in the most general terms. Lebed stresses, however, that any such strategy must reflect

---

[2]"Aleksandr Lebed: 'Russia Won't Survive Another War,'"*Argumenty i fakty*, No. 22, June 1994.

[3]Aleksandr Lebed, "Life Itself Forces Generals to Concern Themselves with Politics," *Izvestiia*, July 20, 1994.

[4]"I'm Not Empowering, But I Have Faith ...," *Soldat Otechestva*, March 13, 1994.

[5]*Argumenty i fakty*, No. 22, June 1994.

[6]Comment on Moscow Russian Television Network, January 24, 1995.

Russia's needs and be designed "for the hearts of the Russian military—not the German, American, or Japanese."[7] Also he has said that any state like Russia which fancies itself a great power "must declare its vital interests as embracing the whole world" and then consider "current, future, and potential" threats to those interests.[8]

ON RECONSTITUTING THE SOVIET UNION

Unlike Vladimir Zhirinovsky, who has left no doubts about his irredentism, and even Communist Party chief Gennady Zyuganov, who also gave the West grounds for concern on this score during his failed campaign to replace Yeltsin, Lebed has conceded that trying to reassemble the USSR is "not only impossible but unnecessary."[9] Nostalgia for bygone times, he admits, is understandable—and even commendable. But it should not be allowed to obstruct a right-minded view of Russia's future and the realistic limits on such a future: "Those who do not mourn the USSR have no heart. But those who dream of rebuilding it have no brain."[10]

Lebed is stoic about the detritus that Russia inherited from failure of communism, conceding that the USSR "was a proper, powerful state which unfortunately collapsed."[11] In his view, the impossibility of reestablishing the union stems in large part from the lack of any de-

---

[7]Interview by Vladimir Kuzmenkin, *Vecherniy Novosibirsk*, April 13, 1995.

[8]Lebed hinted in a casual aside to a reporter that he would not be in any hurry to return the contested northern islands to the Japanese. He said that some Japanese media people had sent him a list of questions, one of which asked whether he would give back the Kuril Islands if he became president: "I told them to go to. . . ." Interview by Vitaly Knyazov, *Sobesednik*, April 1995, p. 3.

[9]Interview by Dimitrina Gergova, "General Lebed: Chechnya Was a Rake on the Path and We Stepped on It," *Trud* (Sofia), July 25, 1995. In a subsequent statement prepared for American consumption, Zyuganov declared outright that his party saw "the restoration of the union of the former Soviet peoples—based on voluntary association—as a historical necessity dictated by Russia's needs and those of world security." See Gennady A. Zyuganov, "'Junior Partner'? No Way," *New York Times*, February 1, 1996.

[10]Interview by Roberto Livi, "I, General Lebed, Will Be Russia's de Gaulle," *Il Messagero* (Rome), December 12, 1995.

[11]Interview by Antun Masle, "If I Become Russian President, I Shall Rule According to the General Pinochet Model. He Killed Only 3000 People and Then Brought About a Real Economic Wonder in Chile," *Globus* (Zagreb), February 17, 1995.

sire for such an action on the part of the newly independent states. As he once put it, "several absolute principalities have replaced the former union republics. The chiefs there do not want to share power."

In a muted variant of the Zyuganov line, however, he has said that it might be possible to establish a confederation and integrate the economies of at least some of the former republics, an approach that he said is "dictated by common sense alone."[12] The ultimate trigger for such a development, he suggested, might be a perceived necessity on the part of the leaders of those former republics who could decide in the end that they cannot manage alone: "Within this destroyed house, there have been created small sovereign states with various pretensions and unilateral policies. They do not yet have economies or societies of their own. . . . It is still not known how all this will end and whether they will survive as sovereign states." Accordingly, argues Lebed, it is not unrealistic to talk about a voluntary confederation "between closely related peoples like the Russians, Ukrainians, Belarusians, and Kazakhs. In these countries, half the population is Russian." He has been adamant, though, that any thought of returning to the Russian empire is "nonsense" and that "Russia should become strong and civilized within the current borders."[13] Lebed has declared that the USSR's breakup is "past history" and that the challenge is to work for a strong Russia.

Lebed has nonetheless put the plight of the Russian diaspora at the top of his list of concerns. He indicated to a reporter in the fall of 1994 that the conditions of the 25 million Russians stranded outside the Russian Federation represented "the most important problem of all," and that "Russia must finally take its people under its protection." He seems to have indicated that he would obey the letter of the law with regard to the sovereignty of the former republics if it came to a clash between the interests of the Russian minorities and that constraint. When pressed, he conceded that the protection of those interests did not "unconditionally" require the use of force. Yet he also insisted that it made no sense to pull Russian troops out of the former republics before Russian citizens were given firm social

---

[12]Interview by Andrzej Rybak, *Die Woche* (Hamburg), December 1, 1995.
[13]Ibid.

guarantees.[14] How Lebed might act now that this issue is his to deal with is a key uncertainty and constitutes valid ground for Western hedging with respect to his current influence and future ambition.

ON RUSSIA AND THE WEST

Lebed has accepted that the cold war is over. He concedes that the fall of the Berlin Wall was "an act of common sense" and that he felt no nostalgia for the Warsaw Pact, since the latter "was an artificially created organization, an alliance based on coercion instead of goodwill. The allies were unwilling."[15]

His main concern in the post–cold war period is Russia's being marginalized. Asked last year how the West can help, Lebed replied: "The West must not isolate us. One cannot isolate one-eighth of the world—this is Russia's size—even if one would like to." He added: "One should not help Russia out of love. One must help Russia to help oneself."

Lebed has commented that Russia's "partnership" with the West (his term) "has progressed so far that it makes isolation impossible," and that "it is the duty of all of Europe not to allow Russia to sink into civil war."[16] Should Russia become isolated, he has warned, "everything here may become completely unpredictable. . . . The West must help, out of pure egotism. And it must help with all available political and financial means."

Such professions suggest that Lebed is not xenophobic and is ready to see Russia join the world as an accepted power. He has not expressed an opinion on the subject of Russian-American military-to-military contacts. He has, however, suggested that he cannot "exclude that the [Russian] military will be integrated into international military-political systems" and that this "will make a great con-

---

[14]Cited in S. G. Simonson, "Going His Own Way: A Profile of General Aleksandr Lebed,"*Journal of Slavic Military Studies*, September 1995, p. 540.

[15]Interview by Dimitrina Gergova, "General Lebed: Russia Is an Empire," *Trud*, (Sofia), July 26, 1995.

[16]Interview by Bela Anda, "Is That the Man Who Will Topple Yeltsin?" *Bild* (Hamburg), February 21, 1995.

tribution to international security."[17] That would seem to indicate that he would be amenable to continued American efforts to engage the Russian armed forces in dialogue and other activities aimed at enlisting them in the common cause of global security.

The big unanswered question in his mind is whether the West really wants this. Lebed has frankly professed his belief that the West is not deeply interested in whether Russia becomes a functioning democracy, and that it only desires, at bottom, for Russia "not to be a nuisance."[18] This indicates an area where more focused U.S. outreach toward Lebed might yield significant payoffs now that he is in a position to have a major say in determining the direction and content of Russian-American relations. Rightly or wrongly, Lebed foresees the coming century as one that will witness a further redrawing of political boundaries around the world. He has voiced concern that a richly endowed yet weakened Russia could become a major prey.[19] The message that he and other concerned Russians need to hear from the United States and its allies is that while we cannot fix Russia's problems, neither are we the cause of its problems or opposed to its recovery as a cooperative player in world affairs.

Where Lebed would draw the line uncompromisingly would be at any gestures by Western governments, irrespective of their purity of motive, that smacked of outside interference in Russian family matters. He was sharply critical in the fall of 1994, for example, of what he regarded as unwelcome interference by the American ambassador to the United Nations in the continuing civil unrest in Moldova.[20] Lebed was also put off by suggestions proffered by a visiting delegation from the Conference on Security and Cooperation in Europe (CSCE) regarding possible ways of ramping down the unpleasantness in Moldova. He commented that "the CSCE representatives worked out their things, signed, suggested, and left. And who will carry it out? . . . The mice agreed that it was time to hang a bell on the cat's

---

[17]Interview by Wierd Duk and Aleksandr Zhilin, "Do I Look Like Pinochet? No, and I Do Not Like His Methods," *Elsevier* (Amsterdam), March 10–11, 1995, pp. 52–53.

[18]Interview by Juan Cicero, *ABC* (Madrid), October 29, 1995.

[19]ITAR-TASS, Moscow, December 14, 1995.

[20]Carey Goldberg, *Los Angeles Times,* January 9, 1995.

tail, but the question remained: Who will do the job?"[21] He has bridled frequently at what he considers the West's growing tendency to treat Russia dismissively as a third-world country.

Lebed is not nearly so vitriolic as Zhirinovsky when it comes to the imperatives of Russian nationalism. But he maintains that Russia has supplicated itself since the collapse of Soviet communism to a point where "the West now believes it can dictate Russia's policies as a natural right. It would be good for the West to remember that, under pressure, Slavic resistance becomes ten times stronger."[22] He objected in particular to American efforts to force Russia to withdraw its 14th Army from Moldova, portraying that as evidence of an underlying desire to "play the role of world gendarme."[23]

Interestingly, against this backdrop of occasional testiness toward the United States, Lebed has warmly acknowledged his personal regard for Colin Powell. "It would be great," he said during his campaign, "if one day I was sitting in the Kremlin and Colin Powell in the White House." Lebed met General Powell in 1991 when the latter was chairman of the Joint Chiefs of Staff and Lebed was the airborne division commander in Tula. Later, Lebed declared: "Powell knows the price of life and the price of blood. As professionals, we hate war most of all. All wars are started by people who never had to serve, by people who know their children and their grandchildren would not be participating." Perhaps the common link here, in the observation of an American reporter, is that Powell and Lebed both "project incorruptibility to two societies that have come to doubt the morality and honesty of their political leaders."[24]

Lebed will probably keep his counsel with respect to the stalled Russian ratification of the Strategic Arms Reduction Treaty (START) II. He has more than once highlighted the central role of Russia's nuclear posture as the nation's last line of defense and has warned that "if, through certain agreements, we lose the nuclear shield, we will

---

[21]Quoted in "Necessary New Policies," *Rossiiskaia gazeta*, March 16, 1994.

[22]Henriette Schroeder, *Suddeutsche Zeitung* (Munich), February 4, 1995.

[23]Sonni Efron, *Los Angeles Times*, June 2, 1995.

[24]Jim Hoagland, "The Challenge of the Generals," *Washington Post*, October 12, 1995.

simply be turned into a doormat."[25] The U.S. Senate's ratification of START II has put the ball in the Duma's court. With Lebed now the chief Russian security planner, he could well be a heel-dragger, if not an outright obstructionist, with regard to START II ratification. The new Russian defense minister, Colonel General Rodionov, is also said to have reservations about whether Russia got an even break in START II.

---

[25]Interview by Aleksandr Prokhanov, "Aleksandr Lebed: 'Strike With a Fist!'" *Zavtra,* August 1995, pp. 1–3.

Chapter Five

THE EXTERNAL SECURITY ENVIRONMENT

Lebed is not paranoid by inclination, and he does not see enemies to the new Russia lurking under every rock. Yet he conforms well to the adage expressed by Lord Salisbury at the Congress of Berlin in 1878 that "if you believe the doctors, nothing is wholesome; if you believe the theologians, nothing is innocent; if you believe the soldiers, nothing is safe."[1]

As chief security adviser to Yeltsin, Lebed will not be looking for trouble around the world. He has insisted, however, on a strong defense posture both as a necessary trademark of great-power status and as a prudent hedge against future uncertainty. "A great power," he has stated, "has always been tied to a strong military. It isn't necessary to fight, but the presence of such a military is a guarantee of the security of the Fatherland."[2] Lebed has been especially voluble on the issue of NATO enlargement. He has also spoken of other threats facing the country.

ON NATO EXPANSION

Lebed's first pronouncement on the NATO enlargement issue was a bald assertion that if Poland and other East European countries are let in, "there will be a World War III that will bury everyone under its rubble." That was hyperbole, and it is highly doubtful that Lebed

---

[1]Quoted in Alfred Vagts, *A History of Militarism*, New York, The Free Press, 1967, p. 362.

[2]*Argumenty i fakty*, No. 22, June 1994.

meant it. His real concern, like that of most others in the Russian defense establishment, is that NATO is, by its nature, a military alliance directed against something, in this case Russia. "Once a bloc exists," he said, "this means there is a potential enemy, and it is assumed that one day, sooner or later, you will come to grapple with him."[3]

In the same interview, Lebed stated that "every military bloc is aimed in some direction, against someone." With respect to NATO, he asked, "who is this enemy? If it is China, then the bloc should be in another part of the world. If the enemy is in Europe, then who can be NATO's enemy—the Czechs, Bulgarians, or Poles? That is ridiculous. . . . There is only one obvious enemy, and that is Russia."

Lebed has often insisted, quite correctly, that NATO remains a military alliance in an era in which its original rationale has vanished. "If you take the military framework out of the military-political bloc called NATO," he declared, "only political junk will be left. A concrete fist is aimed at a concrete adversary."

Lebed does not quarrel with NATO's right to exist, but he questions its purpose and the motivation behind its urge to expand. He once suggested wryly that the Yeltsin government ought to erect a statue of George Bush on the now-empty pedestal of the former Felix Dzerzhinskii monument in front of the KGB's headquarters and affix a placard to it stating: "To the winner of the cold war." Said Lebed: "He would look good there. He did win it. Everybody agrees to this. So why now? Confrontation with whom?"[4]

Like many Russians, Lebed has trouble understanding why the Western allies seem unwilling to let sleeping dogs lie now that they have won the cold war. As he once remarked, almost plaintively: "There used to be two systems. . . . We were ready for combat, and so were they. Then, all of a sudden, one of the systems collapsed, and the Warsaw Pact collapsed with it. . . . Only NATO was left. They were the victors in the cold war. It seems to me that they should have wiped the sweat off their brows, taken a rest, and begun spending

---

[3]Interview by Aleksandr Prokhanov, *Zavtra*, August 1995, pp. 1–3.

[4]Interview by Vladimir Kuzmenkin, *Vecherniy Novosibirsk*, April 13, 1995.

their money on more sensible things. However, nothing like that occurred. Not only did they not disarm, they intend to expand."

On the important question of NATO's post–cold war future, Lebed has suggested that the West might consider as an interim measure honoring the cardinal rule of Hippocrates: "First do no harm." Any precipitous enlargement of NATO, he insists, would violate that rule. He has likened the movement to expand NATO, as an answer to the new security needs of Europe, to brain surgery performed with a chisel. He has similarly likened NATO's involvement in Bosnia to that of "a bull in a china shop."[5] He objects strongly to NATO's seeking to play a role as "the world's policeman who has the right to do anything." Because he is wary of NATO's ultimate intent, he also distrusts the Partnership for Peace: "I don't believe one word of it."[6]

To illustrate his concern, Lebed once observed that Chancellor Helmut Kohl enjoys "great respect and will go down in Germany's history as the man who reunified the nation." He pointedly asked, however, "what assurance is there that some day someone else may not appear who will also want to leave his mark on history? . . . The same Germany now has Kohl. But 50 years ago it had Hitler."[7] Lebed has warned that if NATO expands eastward, "the laws of physics will come into force. Action will be followed by reaction. . . . The NATO bloc will be countered by a new bloc." He has also warned that Russia might abrogate existing arms control treaties and "return to the tactic of nuclear deterrence. Our nuclear shield is still one of the best. It is the only thing for which the West still respects us."[8] Lest one dismiss that as merely an isolated opinion, former defense minister Grachev is on record as having said the same thing—and in even stronger terms.[9] This points to a gathering consensus among main-

---

[5]Agence France-Presse, September 19, 1995.

[6]Interview by Inna Rogatshi, "Aleksandr Lebed's Alternative for Russia: A Moderate Patriot," *Suomen Kuvalehti* (Helsinki), September 8, 1995, pp. 17–20.

[7]Interview by Dimitrina Gergova, *Trud*, (Sofia), July 26, 1995.

[8]Interview by Andrzej Rybak, *Die Woche* (Hamburg), December 1, 1995.

[9]In a speech to cadets and faculty at the Ukrainian Armed Forces Academy in early January, Grachev asserted that any uncompensated NATO expansion eastward might compel Russia to deploy countervailing forces "adequate to the new real threats." Grachev added that "we will have to review our approach to the role and place of tactical nuclear weapons and revise our commitments under military agreements."

stream Russian security professionals that the NATO enlargement school cannot afford to ignore.

More recently, Lebed has engaged the NATO enlargement issue with greater equanimity, and even dismissiveness. During a meeting organized by U.S. Ambassador William Pickering at Spaso House in Moscow with 15 Russian opposition politicians, President Clinton commented that he understood that all assembled there were opposed to NATO enlargement. Alone among them, Lebed gruffly retorted: "Not me."[10] Following his appointment as Yeltsin's security adviser, Lebed intimated that NATO's leaders themselves would soon enough come to realize that they were buying a pig in a poke: "We will find ways of bringing to the attention of the British and American taxpayers the fact that the creation and improvement of military infrastructure in the Baltic countries will cost them roughly $100 billion. . . . So if you have enough money and energy to expand, feel free."[11] A week later, he flatly added that the prospect of NATO expansion "does not bother me" and that he would find a way to persuade same said taxpayers, along with those in France and Germany, of the pointlessness of "paying absolutely enormous sums of money to sustain a raised fist against thin air [i.e., Russia]."[12]

In pursuing this new line, Lebed has assumed a clever stance. Rather than being frontally critical of NATO enlargement, he has asked the United States and its allies, in effect: "Have you guys really thought this through?" This does not mean that he has now become indifferent to NATO expansion. Nevertheless, he is the first senior establishment figure in Moscow to acknowledge Russia's limited ability, at least today, to do anything about it besides complain.

He left the issue with a warning that "everyone must be prepared for preemptive military and political steps to meet possible challenges." Interfax, Moscow, January 4, 1996.

[10]Lee Hockstader, "Can Yeltsin's New Security Czar End the War in Chechnya?" *Washington Post,* June 19, 1996.

[11]ITAR-TASS World Service, Moscow, June 18, 1996.

[12]Quoted in Valery Begishev, "A Union of Two Politicians," *Lesnaia gazeta,* June 25, 1996.

ON OTHER POTENTIAL THREATS

Beyond NATO expansion, Lebed has identified Islamic fundamentalism as a growing challenge to Russian security, fed in part by past errors made by the USSR and perpetuated by the Yeltsin government. Lebed adds that "a third potential enemy is China. They already have a population of 1.2 billion. By the year 2010, they will have an estimated 1.6 billion. And they are already quietly developing our Far East. All this may end up in a severe confrontation." Elsewhere, he remarked: "I respect the Chinese. But they are so many, and they are becoming ever more numerous."[13]

The remaining threats in Lebed's hierarchy of concerns are internal and are topped by the vacuum created by Russia's failure so far to formulate and articulate its national interests. Close behind is the asserted "capitulation policy" vis-à-vis foreign countries which that vacuum has encouraged. These are followed by crime and corruption, mass poverty, waves of refugees, and the plundering of the country's resources. To address these problems, the Congress of Russian Communities party platform for last year's parliamentary elections included several planks which Lebed almost surely had a hand in drafting. Among them were ensuring Russia's restoration to status as a world power; opposing NATO expansion and "the gradual economic and cultural ouster of Russia to the periphery of world politics"; funding the continued development of nuclear forces as the ultimate guarantor of the security and territorial integrity of the state; and supporting the high-technology nucleus of Russia's military-industrial complex.[14]

---

[13]Interview by Michael Winiarski, "Several Threats to Russia's Security," *Dagens Nyheter* (Stockholm), November 26, 1995.

[14]*Kongress Russkikh obshchin: Platforma izbiratelnogo obyedineniya*, September 9, 1995, p. 12.

Chapter Six

THE MILITARY AND SOCIETY

Despite his flamboyance, Lebed has struck a pose of committed professionalism in his public demeanor over the past three years and has projected an aura of being a mud-on-the-boots soldier with a deep sense of loyalty to men in uniform and the right cause. He comes across as a stern disciplinarian, yet not a martinet. And like nearly all senior officers who have spent most of their careers in operational rather than headquarters assignments, he is focused mainly on the mission rather than on palace politics and the bureaucratic process.

It is this background and this mindset that have molded his views on the Russian military and its current predicament. Particularly over the past year, he has been outspoken on the dilapidated state to which the military has fallen, the abuses to which it has been subjected under Yeltsin and Grachev, and its gross misuse in Chechnya and the price this is likely to exact over the long haul. He has also given some strong hints of the military reforms he will pursue now that he has been given both the opportunity and the mandate.

ON THE HEALTH OF THE MILITARY

Unlike the headquarters types in Moscow (often disparaged by field officers as the "Arbat Military District" because of the defense ministry's location at the east end of the Old Arbat pedestrian mall), Lebed takes a grassroots view of the military's situation. He agrees that its problems did not begin overnight but rather have their roots in the bloated and corrupt final days of the Soviet regime. The situation in the post-Soviet Russian armed forces, however, is substantially worse in his view. Centralized command, he maintains, had disappeared in the Soviet military by 1988. What emerged in its place was "an army of lackeys" operating according to the slogans "do not be smart, do not be willful, do not be competent. Be flexible, say 'Yessir!' on every occasion, hang onto the boss's every word, and everything will be fine. There will be a shower of stars on your shoulderboards, and the corresponding positions."

Partly, Lebed argues, these problems are a by-product of the excessively hasty withdrawal of Soviet forces from Eastern Europe and the former Soviet republics. Other parts of the explanation include the catastrophic cuts in defense spending since the USSR's collapse and parallel efforts to convert the military-industrial complex to civilian production. Lebed grants that the withdrawal of Soviet forces from Eastern Europe was unavoidable. But he insists that it was done in an unseemly manner, especially in Germany, from which the Russian military "left like a beaten dog, where our grandfathers had come as victors."[1]

Lebed rightly characterizes Russia's military as a mirror of society and an institution whose great weakness is that only the lowest-quality people—typically of a sort "who have porridge in their heads"—are now being inducted because of the failed conscription system.[2] For its part, the high command is like an upside-down wedding cake, teeming with bosses who are surrounded by concentric rings of eager yes-men. As a case in point, Lebed singled out Grachev's since-dismissed executive assistant Colonel General Valery Lapshov, who assertedly performed "the work of a warrant officer, because his only responsibilities [were] to slice the sausage, pour the vodka, and make sure there's steam in the *banya*." Beneath these multiple layers of higher-headquarters supervision, says Lebed, the army has become "a collection of units and formations without any meaning."[3]

---

[1] Interview by Rodrigo Fernandez, "They Threw Us Russians Out Like Mangy Dogs," *El Pais* (Madrid), September 11, 1994.

[2] "Aleksandr Lebed: 'The Army Is a Mirror of Society—and It's Useless to Upbraid It,'" *Nezavisimaia gazeta*, September 15, 1994.

[3] Interview by Aleksandr Prokhanov, *Zavtra*, August 1995, pp. 1–3.

Clearly pained by the pitiable condition and squalid life that have befallen the armed forces since the collapse of Soviet communism, Lebed attributes these as well to a combination of underfunding and pervasive corruption. In his words: "It is horrible and bitter to admit, but Russia doesn't have an army any more. It only has toy soldiers, formations of boys with no fighting capability."[4] He adds: "I'm sick of serving in an army that is known more and more as a thieves' army. Such an army has no right to exist."[5] In September 1994, he foresaw a 50-percent chance of an outright rebellion by disaffected soldiers who had had enough.

ON THE WAR IN CHECHNYA

Lebed fought in Afghanistan and there observed at first hand the myriad errors committed by the Soviet high command. He sees the war in Chechnya as nearly a mirror-image replay of that earlier misadventure. In his assessment, the Chechen debacle reflects "the whole cesspool, the whole trouble, the whole horror of what has happened to the military and the state. Nobody has analyzed the Afghan war, let alone the Chechen one. Such an analytical approach is absent in the military." Lebed adds: "Historically, it always happens in our country that the military prepares for the last war, without drawing any conclusions from the preceding one. Afghanistan, for instance, demonstrated the complete ineffectiveness of these kinds of preparations, when political goals are murky and vague and the military ones are unachievable altogether, and when a regimental commander would get a Hero of the Soviet Union award for 'exemplary conduct of regimental maneuvers.' It was a complete joke."[6]

Yet again in Chechnya, said Lebed, the "top-heavy and castrated" Russian military was forced by ill preparation and incompetence to prevail by numbers rather than skill. There was no coordination: "In one group of forces, aviation flies on its own. And if we look at the relationship between the army and the MVD [the forces of the sepa-

---

[4]Quoted in Michael Specter, "For Russia's Army, Humbling Days," *New York Times*, January 8, 1995.

[5]Quoted in Carey Goldberg, *Los Angeles Times*, January 9, 1995.

[6]Interview by Aleksandr Prokhanov, *Zavtra*, August 1995, pp. 1–3.

rate Ministry of Internal Affairs], there is practically no interaction at all." On top of that, the war was a classic example of ill-advised planning. "Only an idiot," said Lebed, would have made the decision to start it in winter. He further saw in Chechnya a reprise of the discredited Soviet policy of unit substitution employed in Afghanistan, with "barely experienced people being replaced by those who have seen war only on television."[7]

Lebed views the war in Chechnya as a reflection of the prevailing ills of Russian society and has commented that it signifies, in effect, a civil war on Russian soil. He has voiced genuine concern about the risk of horizontal escalation, noting that the longer the fighting lasts, the greater the chance that the neighboring province of Dagestan will be drawn into the conflict. He has further warned that if left unchecked, it could be a precursor to a serious showdown between Russia and several regional Muslim states.

Lebed has repeatedly described Moscow's entanglement in Chechnya as the result of a refusal by Russia's leaders to learn from history. Those in charge, he said, "failed to take into account the mentality of mountain peoples, their dislike of aggression, the religious factor, winter weather, and unsound analogy when we started an adventure in Afghanistan fifteen years ago." He added that it was time to quit lying about the "perfect execution of this operation and someone's heroic actions. . . . It may sound amazing, but all the mistakes Soviet troops made in Afghanistan have been repeated in Chechnya. The army totally ignored local conditions, religion, and customs. No one planned the operation. It was started 'Russian style' on the off-chance it would work."[8]

Indeed, Lebed has characterized the war as a Russian national disgrace. Never before, he maintains, has the army been so humiliated by the mindless and hamfisted decisions of its leaders. In darker moments, he has even suggested that forces around Yeltsin conjured up the invasion "in an attempt to then call a state of emergency in

---

[7]Interview by I. Morzharetto and V. Perushkin, "I Serve As I See Fit," *Argumenty i fakty,* No. 14, April 1995, p. 3.

[8]Quoted in Michael Specter, *New York Times,* January 8, 1995.

the entire country" as a pretext for canceling the June 1996 presidential election.[9]

With the war less than a month old, Lebed declared that troops from his 14th Army would not fight in Chechnya "under any circumstances."[10] He added that he himself would agree to lead the operation only if it were to involve a complete withdrawal of Russian forces from Chechnya.[11] He said that he would obey an order to "capture that wretched city" [of Grozny] only "provided I was given a regiment entirely composed of the sons of those politicians who, from their lofty positions in the Kremlin, decided to go to war as if it were a fishing trip."

Lebed has stated that Russia's only acceptable option for extricating itself from the Chechnya mess is to stop the killing immediately, withdraw all Russian forces, and evacuate any Russian minorities desirous of leaving. To be sure, he had lost no love for the late Chechen leader Dzhokar Dudayev, who was killed in a precision Russian air attack earlier this year. He has further stated that the rebels should be separated from those Chechens "whose only guilt was to be living there. The situation should have been handled with special forces, concentrating on specific individuals." Yet he has also said that Moscow has no other viable choice than to emulate the United States in Vietnam two decades ago and "declare the Chechens the victors and pack our bags. And move on."[12] The proper way to have dealt with Dudayev, in his opinion, was to have imposed an embargo, controlled the border, and negotiated at the same time.[13] Instead, said Lebed, the Russian army was sent into Chechnya "as if it were going to a banquet." His proposed solution? "If the Chechens want to secede, let them—on tough but civilized conditions that would require them to bear all the burdens of an in-

---

[9]Interview by Wierd Duk and Aleksandr Zhilin, *Elsevier* (Amsterdam), May 10–11, 1995, p. 53.

[10]Interfax, Moscow, December 28, 1994.

[11]Ibid.

[12]Interview by Michel Peyrard, *Paris Match*, February 9, 1995, pp. 58–59.

[13]Interview by Antun Masle, *Globus* (Zagreb), February 17, 1995.

dependent state. I think Chechnya would say, 'No, thank you, we can't do it.'"[14]

Lebed did admit, however, that the Chechen experience held out useful learning value to the Russian military, and that the latter could emerge from the war better off: "We can often benefit from hitting ourselves in the face. It helps one sober up."[15] He also pointed out that as unprepared as the war had revealed the Russian armed forces to be, part of their failure was simply a consequence of incredibly stupid planning.[16] Lebed cautioned that the world should not make too much of the military's poor performance in Chechnya: "The fact that a military organization which has not been given a clearly formulated task cannot take a city, he said, does not signify anything." As to this last statement, considering his ample military experience and insight, Lebed surely knows better.

With Russia still neck-deep in Chechnya, Lebed was recently delivered a golden opportunity to make good on his campaign pledge to end the war by negotiating a resolution that might stop the killing and allow both sides to emerge with honor. On July 10, one of Russia's top on-scene commanders, Major General Nikolai Skripnik of the Interior Ministry forces, was killed when his armored vehicle drove over a mine.[17] Shortly thereafter, the June 1 ceasefire broke down as Russian ground and air units resumed offensive operations against the Chechen rebels. On August 6, rebel forces counterattacked in strength and eventually retook the capital city, killing hundreds of Russian troops in the process, in what has since come to be

---

[14]Quoted in Andrew Nagorski, "The General Waiting in the Wings," *Newsweek*, February 6, 1995. Lebed later embellished this point by noting that "Chechnya is a unique republic. They've been at war with us for 100 years and they haven't concluded a peace. . . . We don't have relations like that with any other republic. And another thing, when Chechnya is left without Russia's handouts, it will be such an example for the others that absolutely nobody else will secede. Like it was with the union republics—they were all eager to go, and now they don't know how to crawl back." "General Lebed: 'Maybe I Should Accept Minister of Culture?!'" *Komsomolskaia pravda*, May 30, 1996.

[15]Interview by Isabella Ginor in *Ha'aretz* (Tel Aviv), January 6, 1995.

[16]For further discussion, see the chapter entitled "Russia's Air War in Chechnya," in Benjamin S. Lambeth, *Russia's Air Power at the Crossroads*, Santa Monica, California, RAND, MR-623-AF, 1996, pp. 191–234.

[17]Reuters dispatch, July 11, 1996.

called the Second Battle of Grozny. That launched Lebed on a three-week roller coaster ride of shuttle diplomacy with the rebel commander, General Aslan Maskhadov, and high-stakes politics with both his army peers and the Yeltsin leadership apparatus in Moscow. The outcome of these efforts appears promising but, so far at least, by no means certain (see Chapter Nine for further discussion).

At this writing, it remains to be seen how Lebed will ultimately fare in handling this daunting challenge both to his near-term prospects as a Yeltsin administration insider and to his longer-term chances of replacing Yeltsin as Russia's president. Before the resumption of fighting in Grozny, he had backpedaled somewhat on the question of a referendum, saying that Chechnya is an inseparable part of Russia and that his earlier call for a plebiscite represented his view while he was a presidential candidate; in his present capacity, he was bound to uphold the policy of the president.[18] He intimated a month before the outbreak of renewed fighting, however, that Chechnya will not, in the end, seek to leave Russia, since "Chechnya needs Russia more than Russia needs Chechnya."[19] Since then, evidently emboldened by his successes to date, he has made a referendum a central part of his long-term peace plan (again, see Chapter Nine for more details).

ON THE POLITICAL ROLE OF THE MILITARY

Lebed has stated baldly that the military has no place in the political process and that the militarization of state structures is "abnormal and brings with it the danger that political conflicts will be settled with weapons."[20] He has been ambivalent, however, with regard to political involvement by individuals within the military. On the one hand, he refused to take sides in the 1991 and 1993 coup attempts. Although he defied the plotters and supported Yeltsin in 1991, Lebed distanced himself from the reformers and declined their efforts to

---

[18]Earlier, Lebed had argued that Russia should "hold a referendum and ask the people of Chechnya what they think on this subject [of secession from the Russian Federation], and if such is their will let them go in peace. We will be good neighbors." Quoted in Valery Begishev, "A Union of Two Politicians," *Lesnaia gazeta*, June 25, 1996.

[19]Interview on Russian Public Television First Channel Network, July 1, 1996.

[20]Interview by Wierd Duk and Aleksandr Zhilin, *Elsevier* (Amsterdam), May 10–11, 1995, p. 53.

enlist his involvement, declaring that "I'm not ready to pretend to be a pseudo-democrat."[21]

He was later approached by both sides in the October 1993 showdown. He shunned Aleksandr Rutskoi, whom Lebed said had treated him with gratuitous and unwarranted condescension ("with humans, I conduct myself in a human manner. With swine like a swine.")[22] He also declined a more solicitous entreaty from the Yeltsin side, on the premise that he was a serving officer who owed his loyalty solely to the people and the state. Lebed has argued that political involvement by men in uniform is corrosive to order and discipline: "Imagine a tank with the commander a communist, the gunner a democrat, and the engineer an agrarian. This does not work."[23]

On the other hand, Lebed has insisted that it is wholly acceptable for generals to play in politics, on the ground that Russia's domestic situation is in sufficient disarray to warrant such an extraordinary practice for a professional military institution. He argued that in a "civilized" state, one cannot force the military into politics "even with a stick. But it's another case here, where every question is a political one."[24]

Expanding on this, he later said that "in a civilized country, the military has nothing to do with politics. But that applies in a normal country that understands that the military is an institution that must be protected and funded. In Russia, unfortunately, all problems become political. . . . So whether I like it or not, the military is becoming politicized." The reason for this, explained Lebed, is that the army is no longer performing its primary function of training and configuring to defend the state. Lebed conceded that the Russian officer corps had no tradition of military coups. But to a question of

---

[21]"The 'Favorite' of Pridniestria—A Maker of Enemies," *Moskovskii komsomolets*, June 4, 1994.

[22]*Soldat Otechestva*, March 13, 1994.

[23]Interview by Andrzej Rybak, *Die Woche* (Hamburg), December 1, 1995.

[24]*Izvestiia*, July 20, 1994.

whether the time might come in the future when the army would be forced to seize power, he replied: "Who knows?"[25]

Much of this ambivalence during his earlier days of political life may have reflected Lebed's own frustrations and personal career as it evolved from his assignment to Moldova in 1992 to his departure from military service last year. His party platform, however, was crystal-clear on the matter, calling for an end to the abuse of the military and its involvement in domestic politics, and banning through legislation any use of the military for performing police functions within the country. That was the signal that mattered most.[26] It indicated that at bottom Lebed sees the proper role of the military as solely the defense of the state against external aggression. "The army," he declared after the June presidential election, "simply must be positioned with its back to the country and its face to the border."[27]

ON GRACHEV AND THE MILITARY LEADERSHIP

Lebed served twice under Grachev, once in Afghanistan and later as deputy airborne forces commander. In both cases, Grachev was Lebed's patron. Grachev also was Lebed's platoon commander when both were cadets at the Ryazan Higher Airborne Forces Academy. Lebed maintains that he always had good working relations with Grachev, but never a friendship. His disenchantment with his former sponsor began when he saw from the grassroots the cynicism of Moscow's generals, the corruption at high echelons tolerated by Grachev, and the failure of Grachev to pursue reforms of real consequence. Lebed has commented that the dark side of power is amply demonstrated by what happens when people of Grachev's alleged moral bankruptcy attain power so quickly. He voiced special contempt for Grachev's hand-picked deputy defense minister, Matvei Burlakov, as a corrupt officer and bad example, adding that as long as he was still 14th Army commander, he would never permit

---

[25]Interview by Rodrigo Fernandez, *El Pais* (Madrid), September 11, 1994.

[26]*Kongress Russkikh obshchin: Platforma izbiratelnogo obyedineniya*, p. 12.

[27]Radio Station *Ekho Moskvy*, Moscow, June 20 1996.

General Burlakov to make an inspection visit to Transdniestria: "I do not welcome thieves here."[28]

Lebed later declared that Burlakov's firing by Yeltsin on grounds of corruption was "a triumph for justice" and that "Grachev must [also] go, if only to safeguard the honor of the army and its morale." For his part, Grachev defended Burlakov angrily and warned that if the latter were exonerated of corruption charges, Lebed would be dismissed from service for defaming a fellow officer. In turn, Lebed called for Grachev to resign, accusing him of presiding over the military's decay instead of reforming it.

No serving officer in any military can speak this way of his superior openly and expect to endure for long, as Lebed was soon to learn. Still undaunted and unabashed, Lebed further remarked that too many of the Russian military's current leaders are armchair generals: "There is nothing more dangerous than generals who have not seen war. Generals without war experience, especially those who don't know the smell of gunpowder, and who with unusual ease unleash all kinds of conflicts in hope of an elusive victory."[29]

The onset of the war in Chechnya added a powerful impetus to Lebed's excoriation of Grachev. He holds Grachev personally responsible for having let the military get sucked in and needlessly discredited. Regarding the inept strategy that underlay the invasion, Lebed declared with sarcasm that Grachev was "undoubtedly a wise man, perhaps even the best defense minister of all time. He has succeeded by barbaric bombing raids in turning indifferent civilians into fanatical soldiers."[30] He further implied that Grachev had been willingly and knowingly duped by his political bosses: "There is not a single known case in history of a general getting up on the wrong side of the bed one morning and starting a war. The reasons for the start of a war always emanate from a country's political leadership."[31] Lebed even accused Grachev of having been complicit in arming the

---

[28]Quoted in Simonson, *Journal of Slavic Military Studies,* p. 538.

[29]"To Feel for One's Country" *Krasnaia zvezda,* March 4, 1994.

[30]Interview by Michel Peyrard, *Paris Match,* February 9, 1995.

[31]Interview by I. Morzharetto and V. Perushkin, *Argumenty i fakty,* No. 14, April 1995, p. 3.

Chechen resistance, noting that eventually the minister should be called to answer for that transgression before a war crimes tribunal.[32]

Lest it appear from the foregoing that Lebed set out like some Don Quixote to take on the entire general-officer establishment, he took care to discriminate between Grachev and his clique and other military leaders of more respected character. He has never equated Grachev with the defense ministry and has insisted that he maintains good relations with those higher-headquarters generals who have shown a genuine interest in the military's future and real concern that Grachev's "pseudo-reforms are taking the military down a blind alley."[33] Among the latter, he included Generals Semenov, Vorobyev, Gromov, and Mironov, who he said represent the Russian army's elite, yet, as a sign of the times, are "sadly finding themselves out of business today."[34]

A month before the election, after he was safely out of uniform, Lebed recounted a most unflattering story about how Grachev, while hosting General Powell during his tenure as Soviet airborne commander in the summer of 1991, insisted on going ahead with a large-scale demonstration paradrop in high winds, over Lebed's strong objection, in order to "let General Powell see what Soviet paratroopers can do." As a result of this callous and foolhardy decision, one Soviet jumper was killed and several others sustained severe fractures upon landing, leaving the dumbfounded American general staring at Grachev and allegedly asking: "What are you doing? What are you doing?" Commented Lebed on this embarrassing performance: "Was Powell impressed? No. He is an ordinary man who understands the value of life and blood. He simply was not used to seeing people treated like that."[35]

---

[32]Quoted in Simonson, *Journal of Slavic Military Studies*, p. 539.

[33]In a comment that seemed, in retrospect, almost assured to help hasten his political demise considering the timing, Grachev himself stated less than two months before his dismissal by Yeltsin that the time had not yet come to speak of "deep reform" within the military because of insufficient financial conditions. Interfax, Moscow, May 1, 1996.

[34]Interview with Lebed, "General Lebed Passes Inspection," *Moskovskiye novosti*, No. 7, January 29–February 5, 1995, p. 10.

[35]Election speech by Lebed, Mayak Radio Network, Moscow, May 14, 1996.

MILITARY REFORM NEEDS

Although Lebed has been an outspoken proponent of military reform, he faulted Yeltsin and Grachev early on for going too far in their plans to downsize the Russian defense establishment, insisting that the military's manning level must be commensurate with the size of the country: "One percent of the population is silly. We have a territory of such character that one percent won't do."[36] Lebed has argued that the military's tooth-to-tail ratio should be six combatants to four support personnel.

Like most of Russia's military leaders, he also insists that Russia has little choice but to retain military conscription. As desirable as an all-volunteer army might be in the abstract, Lebed maintains that Russia will not be within reach of one for years because it lacks the money that would be needed to pay for it. He has said that only the United States and Great Britain enjoy the luxury of having such a military, and that "whether we want it or not, we will have to man [ours] with draftees."[37] This may put him head-to-head on the issue with his new president, who made a campaign promise to end the draft by the year 2000.[38]

As for the fallen quality of Russia's military manpower, Lebed said that the army needed to recruit people "who have war in their blood, in their genes, and then it will be a regular host. Because it's abnormal when it takes three people to look after one soldier to make sure he doesn't cut something off, that he doesn't desert, or that his mama doesn't take him away."[39] Furthermore, argues Lebed, only the highest-quality individuals are capable of being properly trained. He proposed that the ultimate measure of merit of a soldier is that he should be able to be awakened in the middle of the night and, before he even opens his eyes, be able to jump into a tank turret, shoot, and hit the target. To attain such a standard requires that he be intensively trained for 22 days a month. Never, warns Lebed, will Russia

---

[36]*Izvestiia*, July 20, 1994.

[37]Interview by Vladimir Kuzmenkin, *Vecherniy Novosibirsk*, April 13, 1995.

[38]Perhaps in a dying bid to retain his job, Grachev enthusiastically endorsed this Yeltsin campaign initiative as "timely and necessary." Interfax, Moscow, May 20, 1996.

[39]Interview by Vitaly Knyazov, *Sobesedenik*, April 1995, p. 3.

produce such a soldier in the face of draft exemptions that spare the most capable from military service, while leaving commanders with "semi-literates and illiterates" in their stead.

Lebed also has stressed that Russia's defense industry must be protected from disintegration. Yet at the same time, he agrees that it must be reduced in size and rendered more efficient, citing as a case in point that Russia needs at most only three tank plants, not ten. His KRO party platform called for preserving the current five-service structure of the armed forces and creating a unified system of command and control.[40]

Lebed has advocated the creation of smaller, lighter, and more mobile and better trained ground force units, and has urged that Russia's disparate combat forces, including the border guards and Internal Affairs troops, be integrated under the operational command of the General Staff. He has become a vocal proponent of quality over quantity, having recently declared that "if we can't afford to maintain 5000 airplanes, let there be fewer. A modern pilot, especially a highly trained pilot, is as valuable for the air force as a technically superior combat aircraft." He has further conceded that there is no need for Russia to compete with the better-endowed West in arms production and deployment: "It is time to understand that the world has changed. . . . We do not have to keep up with the United States or NATO in terms of quantity." Interestingly, he went on record several days after the June 16 election to state that there is enough money in the current defense allocation to begin a serious program of military reform: "If we use rationally the humble resources that we have at our disposal today, we can improve the situation in the armed forces."[41] How well Lebed will do in adhering to that assurance once the Yeltsin administration establishes its post-election footing remains to be seen.

---

[40]*Kongress Russkikh obshchin: Platforma izbiratelnogo obyedineniya*, p. 12.

[41]Lee Hockstader, "Can Yeltsin's New Security Czar End the War in Chechnya?" *Washington Post*, June 19, 1996.

Chapter Seven

DOMESTIC POLITICS AND SOCIAL PROBLEMS

As one might expect of a career officer who grew up in an insular and repressive military culture, Lebed evinces political views based more on opinion than on any deep or reflective thought. Although his sense of the country's problems and priorities resonates well with the frustrations of the rank and file, he has not yet shown a coherent set of prescriptions for addressing them. His KRO party platform spelled out a philosophy of governance that, on first blush, did not sound alarming or retrogressive. But it is a safe bet that many hands more politically gifted than Lebed's played the major role in drafting it.

Indeed, this may be Lebed's single greatest weakness as a contender for national leadership. He has struck the right chord among the masses by forcefully articulating what is wrong with Russia in terms to which they can easily relate. But he has provided little basis, beyond a superficial litany of appeals and exhortations, for speculation about what he might do to fix things. Instead, he has groped about for colorful role models of the leadership style he would seek to emulate, citing as examples at worst the former Chilean military dictator Augusto Pinochet, and at best France's General Charles de Gaulle.

Yet, in the simplicity of his thinking, one can see in Lebed an underlying sense of the common good and of the obligations of a sheltering society, an implicit grasp of the difference between right and wrong, and an avowed respect for the natural rights of the individual. In this, Lebed is anything but a throwback to Leninism. The unanswered, and perhaps unanswerable, question is whether, now that he has attained a position of real influence in the Russian government, he will practice what he has been preaching—or even know how to do so.

ON THE NEED FOR A STRONG LEADER

Lebed is the dream come true for millions of Russians who have grown fed up with the corruption, disorder, and vanishing quality of life that have been the downside results of Yeltsin's experiment with democracy and who yearn for an iron disciplinarian to take the helm and undo these excesses—by fiat if need be. This is not to say that Lebed believes that the Soviet system which Yeltsin destroyed was superior. Indeed, he has had equally unkind words for the Pandora's box that Gorbachev opened in 1986. Yet like many Russian conservatives, Lebed contends that "the mistakes of the old system were child's play compared to the chaos in which we live now."[1] He has stated that "Russia is crying out for an absolute ruler who will lead it benevolently. Today the country needs a dictatorship of law, a leader who strengthens Russia's condition as a state."[2]

It is this dimension of Lebed's outlook that is most disturbing to many both in Russia and in the West who are leery of giving this insistent populist the benefit of the doubt. In the fall of 1994, Lebed asked an interviewer rhetorically—and ominously: "What's wrong with a military dictator? In all its history, Russia has prospered under the strictest control. Consider Ivan the Terrible, Peter the Great, Catherine the Great, or Stalin."[3]

Lebed has often been cited as a self-professed admirer of the former Chilean dictator Pinochet's take-no-prisoners approach to leadership, in a variation on the notion that you can't make an omelet without breaking eggs: "What did he do? He led the state from total collapse and put the military in first place. . . . Now Chile is a prosperous country. . . . This supports the theory that when one pounds his fist on the table once, a hundred men are put on the altar of the Fatherland and the issue is closed. Or is it better in a situation in

---

[1]Henriette Schroeder, *Suddeutsche Zeitung* (Munich), February 4-5, 1995.

[2]Interview by Andrzej Rybak, *Die Woche* (Hamburg), December 1, 1995.

[3]Quoted in S. G. Simonson, "Going His Own Way: A Profile of General Aleksandr Lebed," *Journal of Slavic Military Studies*, September 1995, p. 543.

which five men die every day, seemingly small potatoes, but in time it adds up to a million?"[4] When challenged with respect to the human rights violations of Pinochet, Lebed replied that he had no choice but to demand a strong hand to rule Russia: "Peter the Great tolerated thieves, but they stole elsewhere and brought their loot back home. Our contemporaries, on the other hand, do their robberies at home and take the loot abroad. Here heads must roll, mercilessly."

Later, Lebed argued that Pinochet was typically disparaged as a butcher and dictator, yet that he also was "an able politician" who killed "only 3000 people" during his 18-year rule and ultimately produced a flourishing Chilean economy. "More people than that are killed here in a day, our economic situation is getting worse from one day to the next, and yet nobody considers our people butchers."[5] Increasingly, however, Lebed has tended to backpedal on this point as well, conceding that he is not an unbridled enthusiast of Pinochet. No doubt this belated footwork has been motivated by a dawning awareness on his part of the tarnish that such a role model could impart to Lebed's populist halo in the eyes of many. He later admitted that he did not admire Pinochet's methods and looked instead to de Gaulle as a more appropriate role model.[6]

This artful shift offers little reassurance to those in the West who are hoping that Russia will weather its current turmoil without falling off a course more or less in the direction of continued reform. As for his notion of the ideal leader, Lebed's bottom line has hitherto been that Russia "has been without stern, sails, and wind, and it needs someone at the helm. We are doomed to live in an authoritarian state until genuine democracy, which should not be confused with anarchy, is set up."[7] With Lebed now ensconced at Yeltsin's side and openly angling to replace him as president, and with better prospects now than ever of doing so, we could soon find out whether he really means this or instead will acquire enduring democratic values

---

[4] *Izvestiia*, July 20, 1994.

[5] Interview by Antun Masle, *Globus* (Zagreb), February 17, 1995.

[6] Interview by Roberto Livi, *Il Messagero* (Rome), December 12, 1995.

[7] Alessandra Stanley, *New York Times*, October 13, 1995.

through his exposure as a cautious bureaucratic politician to the ways of a developing democratic political system.

ON CRIME AND CORRUPTION

A big part of the rationale for Lebed's call for strong leadership is that crime and corruption have gyrated out of control in Russia and that nothing less, in his view, will reverse these excesses of the Yeltsin government's experiment at democratization. Of course, Lebed admits that corruption was systemic under communist rule as well. He once remarked that the top Soviet leaders "had long ceased being communists; they lived in a personal paradise and had everything. And below was a herd of party sheep who went into battle, forged the party's glory, sowed, plowed, did not know anything about privileges, and never had a chance to use them. Fish rots from the head down, and it finally rotted. The building collapsed." He added that this metastasized rot first dawned on him when he was exposed to it directly. The Communist Party, he said, was dominated by "numerous small, petty, minute factions and egoistic aspirations" and was "ruled by senile people, far removed from the people and from reality."[8]

Today, Lebed maintains, Russia's overarching social problem is the absence of a functioning legal system that can enforce domestic order and guarantee civil discipline: "How is corruption possible in Russia? There is no economy, there is a social system without any control, there is complete apathy. . . . The economy should be revived, clear laws should be passed, and problems should not be solved with bribes but with legal remedies. There is no corruption in countries in which a firm legal system functions."[9]

High on Lebed's list of evils is what he calls "nomenklatura capitalism," namely, the flourishing economy set in motion by former high party bureaucrats who simply robbed state funds under their control and privatized them for their own gain. Step one in any campaign to eradicate this abuse of the rank and file by the privileged, says Lebed, is that "every corrupt functionary must be declared a state criminal, starting with the police," whom he dismisses as mere "dec-

---

[8]Interview by Aleksandr Prokhanov, *Zavtra*, August 1995, pp. 1–3.

[9]Interview by Antun Masle, *Globus* (Zagreb), February 17, 1995.

orations."[10]   In an on-target comment, he reported: "Today the criminals have fast cars, automatic weapons, bulletproof vests, and satellite telephones.   They are countered by militiamen who haven't had a paycheck for three months and who are driving Ladas that are falling apart."[11]   He has further railed against the steady encroachment of get-rich-quick values and mafia jargon into the everyday vocabulary of Russia's successor generation: "Our children have already picked up their first words: *Reket* [racket], *krysha* [cover], *babki* [cash], *baksy* [bucks]. . . . We should pass on to them a cleaner heritage."[12]

Lebed would initiate change on this front by moving promptly to reverse what he calls "unfair" privatization by forcing those who have profited by stealing from the state's coffers either to return the money or to lose their mansions and businesses. He has conceded that he would not rescind privatization completely, however. "It must be fair. We are too far away from the shore to swim back."[13]

Later, after the June 16 election, he qualified this comment by saying that "there have been many flaws in privatization, it's true. But there must be no mass redivision of property. Most of the people took guidance from the laws that were in force at the time. To be sure, there have been some deviations. These should be straightened out in a civilized way. If something cost billions but only millions were paid for it, please be so kind as to cover the difference. If you don't want to pay up the difference, then here's your million, and good luck!" As for the banking system, he said that "this is the state's circulatory system. To dismantle it would mean ruining the financial system, and this will lead to the ruin and collapse of the country."[14]

Yet another problem in need of fixing, according to Lebed, is Russia's tax policy, which is at the same time hypocritical and toothless, making honesty a losing game and forcing everyone to cheat.   Tax

---

[10]Interview by Roberto Livi, *Il Messagero* (Rome), December 12, 1995.

[11]Interview by Andrzej Rybak, *Die Woche* (Hamburg), December 1, 1995.

[12]Campaign speech, Mayak Radio Network, Moscow, May 14, 1996.

[13]Ibid.

[14]Interview by Igor Korotchenko, "The Question of a Coalition Government Is on the Agenda," *Nezavisimaia gazeta*, June 18, 1996.

evasion and concealment of income are rampant because taxes are unrealistic and exorbitant, bordering on robbery, in Lebed's view. His solution? Taxes must first be made reasonable, and then payment must be equally enforced at all levels. In another on-target observation, Lebed remarked that if Prime Minister Chernomyrdin's Gazprom (natural gas) empire alone paid its fair share of taxes, the nation's revenue problem would advance a major step toward resolution. That indelicate charge might well prove to be one of many scores Chernomyrdin will try to settle with Lebed now that the two are locked in high-stakes political combat.

With his newly assigned powers as Yeltsin's Security Council chief, Lebed can be expected to lead an all-out war against the decline in morale values and the assault on Russian culture that have been prompted by the nonstop importation of smut and crass materialism from the West ever since the USSR's demise. He has summarized his attitude on this score: "We are frankly being turned into drunkards, spiritually and morally poisoned by the violence-and-sex rubbish that has filled the screens of television sets and theaters."[15] As laudable as this concern may be in principle, Lebed may find acting on it successfully something of an upriver swim because both momentum and diverse financial interests will be working against him.

ON PRESIDENT YELTSIN

At the beginning of his rise to prominence, Lebed was reluctant to speak ill of his commander in chief. When asked by an interviewer early on of his opinion of Yeltsin, he replied: "You lead me into an area in which you force me to violate the principle of subordination if I express an opinion. That is my concern. For better or worse, he is our president."[16] Lebed was less inhibited, however, with another reporter only a few days earlier, when he described the Russian president as "a nullity."[17]

---

[15]Interview by Aleksandr Prokhanov, *Zavtra*, August 1995, pp. 1-3.

[16]Interview by Rodrigo Fernandez, *El Pais* (Madrid), September 11, 1994.

[17]John Lloyd, "Russian Military in Troubled Mood," *Financial Times* (London), September 8, 1994.

In a later amplification on this concern, Lebed stated that "Boris Yeltsin is by nature a wrecker. The only politics he knows involves breaking down and destabilizing his surroundings. That is great in a transitional period, but now it's time to build, and Boris Yeltsin is no builder."[18] As a result of Yeltsin's inability to lead, he added, "Russia is increasingly turning into a ship without a rudder. The situation worsens every minute President Yeltsin stays in power."[19] In a clear swipe at Yeltsin's growing reliance on an inner circle of cronies led by the likes of Korzhakov, Lebed observed that Russia is well endowed with intelligent people and that "the power structure must be made up on the basis of character and competence, not according to personal devotion."

Lebed insists that there has been no "second Russian revolution." Instead, he holds, "a regime which was rotten through and through simply collapsed like an old wooden hut. Yet nothing changed. We went to bed under totalitarianism on August 21 and woke up on August 22 under democracy. However, things don't happen that way." While admittedly a hero of the 1991 coup's undoing, Yeltsin was and remains, in Lebed's view, at bottom little more than an opportunist, who, like most of the smarter apparatchiks, soon knew which way the wind was blowing. In Lebed's disdainful account, "they sized up the situation instantly, threw their party membership cards into the trash can, unfurled the flag of democracy, and set off on their white horses to lead us to a bright future. This future used to be called communism. Now it is called democracy. However, the system has remained the same."

Before his cooptation by the president in the wake of the June 16 election, Lebed charged that the Yeltsinites had permitted uncontrolled privatization in the interest of 5 percent of the population, leaving 80 percent stranded below the poverty line while their leaders have "no guiding star or idea where they are going."[20] He further blamed Yeltsin for the country's descent into chaos, for the 1993 shootout at the White House, for uncontrolled inflation, and for be-

---

[18]Interview by Virginie Coulloudon, "Boris Yeltsin Is a Wrecker," *Le Point* (Paris), February 18, 1995, pp. 54–55.

[19]Interview by Bela Anda, *Bild* (Hamburg), February 21, 1995.

[20]Interview by Dimitrina Gergova, *Trud*, (Sofia), July 26, 1995.

ing driven solely by a desire to "hold onto power to the death."[21] Perhaps revealingly, he contrasted that to what he considered the more exemplary case of China, where an economic explosion has not been accompanied by democratization, thus "proving," in his view at the time, that a revolution is not necessary and that there is no self-evident case for importing foreign experience to Russian soil.

ON ZHIRINOVSKY AND THE COMMUNISTS

Partly out of core conviction and partly to distance himself at the outset from his inflammatory competitor's odious reputation among the literate, Lebed dismissed Vladimir Zhirinovsky as "a dangerous clown" and went out of his way to disavow the latter's lunatic ravings, explaining: "Who would maintain relations with a state whose leaders are scoundrels?"[22] Lebed further insisted that he would "never stand together with the fascists, whatever attractive goals they might proclaim."[23] With respect to Zhirinovsky personally, Lebed has observed that "any madman can make war on his own account" and has insisted that he will "never join forces with a madman like him, even if power should be the reward."[24] Perhaps in a variation on "read my lips" for those tuning in from abroad, he more recently underscored for effect: "I am not Zhirinovsky. The West has nothing to fear, no reason to be afraid."

Lebed has blown hot and cold on the communists. On the one hand, he has declared emphatically that he will have nothing to do with them. Shortly before the election, he portrayed Zyuganov as "a rather weak man in a personal sense" who "looks at the date of June 16 with terror."[25] On the other hand, he has seemingly yielded on this a bit, at least at the margins, in his elliptic suggestion after signing up with Yeltsin that Russia is "fated to have a coalition govern-

---

[21] Ibid.

[22] Interview by Bela Anda, *Bild* (Hamburg), February 21, 1995.

[23] Interview by Ivan Boltovskii, "Conscience Has Become a Luxury Today, and Many People Have Learned to Do Without It," *Pravda-5*, September 29-October 6, 1995, pp. 8–9.

[24] Interview by Juan Cicero, *ABC* (Madrid), October 29, 1995.

[25] Personal interview, "Aleksandr Lebed: My Program Has to Be Explained to Everyone," *Sovetskaia molodezh*, May 21, 1996.

ment" and that everyone must be given a chance "to use the whole power of his party and movement to create good living."[26] More and more, however, the question has become irrelevant as the Yeltsin government continues to struggle fitfully toward consolidating its second term with little need to look over its shoulder any longer at the machinations of its communist opposition.

ON THE PROSPECTS FOR DEMOCRACY

Ever since the first days of his campaigning when he still commanded the 14th Army, Lebed has been darkly pessimistic about the chances for democracy in Russia. He is definitely not a democrat himself, even in the faint sense that Boris Yeltsin may still be, let alone one in the mold of Grigory Yavlinsky or Yegor Gaidar, the two Russian politicians to whom Westerners looked first as beacons of hope. Only Lebed himself can say for sure to what extent he believes democratic reform to be a noble goal for Russia in principle. But he has adamantly insisted: "I have never believed and do not believe in our pseudo-democracy."[27]

If asked to summarize his view in a word, Lebed would probably insist that Russia's democratic experiment has been a failure. On joining KRO, he observed that "over the course of a decade of perestroika, accompanied by gunfire, we accomplished nothing." He added that "we are advancing, unfortunately, toward a dictatorship, because many people in power have embezzled up to their necks and can feel safe only if they remain in power."[28] Lebed maintains that "the West is continuing to support those currently in power in Russia because it refuses to understand that a strong and stable Russia, free of dictatorship and authoritarianism, is safer and more profitable for everyone than a weakened, corrupt Russia which is in a constant

---

[26]As for the other candidates, Lebed described Yeltsin as the most experienced of all the contenders and one whose strength lay mainly in his courage and quest for power. He saw Yeltsin as awaiting the June election "with great sporting excitement." He portrayed Yavlinsky as "a capable person" but one cut out of the wrong material for the job. Russian Public Television First Channel, Moscow, June 30, 1996.

[27] *Soldat Otechestva*, March 13, 1994.

[28]Interfax, Moscow, April 11, 1995.

death struggle."[29] It remains to be seen whether increased contacts with Western officials will lead Lebed, now that he has become a Kremlin insider, to a more informed and sophisticated view on this score.

Whatever the case, the West should not expect much luck in persuading Lebed to abandon his by no means groundless insistence that the very concept of democracy is alien to Russia. "I am convinced," he has said, "that I will not live to see the day when we have real democracy. It has to be built brick by brick, without hurry. It is a colossal task to build up a system of laws that will defend the weak. We Russians have never had a horse on that field." To underscore this, he once cited the analogy of Mikhail Gorbachev's vain attempt to cultivate cactus at his summer dacha: "We have grown an ugly plant not suited to Russia." If pressed, he would probably agree in principle that democracy is desirable. He would counter, however, that for it to truly exist and flourish in Russia will require "a colossal transformation in the people's consciousness and in educating them to observe the laws." This presupposes conditions that will exist only when laws first begin operating in the interest of the majority. Only then, says Lebed, can Russia claim honestly that it has begun laying the foundations of democracy: "Personally, I am convinced that I will not live to see this day."[30]

Lebed was also skeptical at first of Russia's new legislative process, characterizing the Duma as a "submissive organ" that "does not decide anything." He said that "there are many intelligent people there, and many good speakers. But you don't see a lot of statesmen."[31] Amplifying on this, he added that the Duma "bakes laws for itself like pancakes and then throws them out the window. It doesn't care whether this causes anyone harm, because the Duma lacks any controlling function. That lies in the hands of the president." In yet another hint of skepticism, Lebed asked: "How is the Duma financed? From the treasury of the presidential administration. It is well known that he who pays the piper calls the tune."

---

[29]Interview by Wierd Duk and Aleksandr Zhilin, *Elsevier* (Amsterdam), March 10–11, 1995, p. 53.

[30]Interview by Dimitrina Gergova, *Trud* (Sofia), July 26, 1995.

[31]Interview by Vitaly Knyazov, *Sobesednik*, April 1995, p. 3.

All of that, of course, was before Lebed's own election as a parliamentarian on December 17, 1995.   Unfortunately, his mere six months in that role before being tapped to become Yeltsin's security adviser were not enough to acculturate him to a different view of the Duma and its importance to the development of a system of checks and balances in Russia, particularly since he spent most of that time campaigning for president in opposition to Yeltsin.   Now that Lebed occupies a high position in the executive branch, he will have new incentives, simply by virtue of where he sits, to regard the Duma as part of the problem rather than part of the solution.

All in all, however, it is Lebed's inner belief that if democracy is realizable in principle in Russia, it is scarcely around the corner and could take a generation or more to build.   In the meantime, he would argue, one must survive the short run.   Lebed has posited a need for Russian governance to find a place between the would-be democrats, who he insists have botched things royally, and the communists, who in his view lack the capacity to lead.   As he has described this pragmatically, "no matter how long you strive to seek the horizon, you never reach it.   We need to live today with what we have."[32]

---

[32]Excerpt from an interview by Flora Lewis, "He's No Democrat," *Los Angeles Times*, December 15, 1995.

Chapter Eight

LEBED'S LIKELY POLICY AGENDA

Is Lebed a reformer? A democrat? A nationalist? Does he have good political instincts and judgment? These and questions of like import do not yet have unambiguous answers.[1] Lebed has sent mixed signals on many. He is all over the map on some issues, such as NATO enlargement. Beyond the few anecdotal clues he has provided, he remains a blank slate on foreign affairs. Also, he is weak on economics and is a complete novice when it comes to law enforcement, despite his strongly held views on the issue.

The foregoing chapters have sought to sketch out, in as much detail as the evidence will permit, a policy-useful picture of the Aleksandr Lebed who has lately become a factor to be reckoned with in Russian politics. Now that his power is real, what does his presence on the scene imply for Russia and for broader East-West relations?

ISSUES ON THE HOME FRONT

Lebed's domestic agenda is likely to focus on four key problem areas: (1) crime and corruption, (2) the war in Chechnya, (3) the composition and role of the Security Council, and (4) military reform. On the first count, assuming that he does not self-destruct through his own missteps or otherwise become consumed by Kremlin intrigue, he can be expected to try to lend real teeth to the police and to crack down on those Soviet captains of industry and other nomenklatura bosses

---

[1]See "Alexander Lebed, Russia's Dark Swan," *The Economist* (London), June 22, 1996, p. 48.

who have become rich at the expense of the rank and file. This was, after all, a major plank in his campaign platform. The unanswered question is whether broader civil liberties might suffer along the way.

A related question concerns the degree of Lebed's motivation to rekindle the spirit of reform that flashed evanescently under Yeltsin's lead in the wake of the failed 1991 coup. On this score, the outlook is not encouraging. Lebed brings to Russia's leadership an authoritarian personal style developed over many years of military upbringing. He has been critical of what he perceives to be the excesses of glasnost, and he may not countenance unlimited freedom of the press, especially once he becomes a target of its criticism rather than an object of its curiosity and charmed bemusement.[2]

It would, however, be both unfair and inaccurate to brand Lebed an out-and-out reactionary. He exudes unbridled disgust over what the communists stand for and what their failed stewardship did to bring down the USSR.[3] He is prepared to grant that Zyuganov probably personally harbors a social-democratic outlook. But he has been uncompromising in stressing that "those who stand behind him are communists of the Stalinist type. If they should come to power, in all likelihood they will turn the country back" to a Soviet-style dictatorship.[4] He has also sought to put a human face on his own reputation for authoritarianism and to explain it as a trait naturally tied to the responsibilities of his former calling: "To be sure, I'm an authoritarian person because I'm a general and have been entrusted with the heavy and terrible right to send people to their death. But throughout my career, I've tried to make sure that they come back from hell alive."[5]

---

[2]For whatever it may be worth, however, Lebed has said, "God forbid that I should try to encroach on freedom of the press. A free press is perhaps our only gain in recent years." Quoted in Kirill Svetitskii, "Russian Security Now Has Four Aspects, While the Fight Against Crime Will Begin with Finance," *Izvestiia,* July 12, 1996.

[3]Like many senior officers who were put off by the putschists' attempt to involve the military as the sharp end of their reactionary coup, Lebed resigned his party membership in August 1991.

[4]Quoted in Bruce Nelan, "The Undead Red," *Time,* April 8, 1996, p. 37.

[5]Interview with Rodion Morozov, "With Trouser Stripes and Charisma," *Obshchaia gazeta,* November 18–14, 1994, p. 8.

It was surely putting things too enthusiastically by half when journalist Georgie Anne Geyer suggested, after interviewing Lebed last year, that "if Washington had any sense, it would be rooting for him as the only leader who can bring some order to the mess that is Russia today."[6] Yet to his credit, Lebed has repeatedly stressed the indispensability of the rule of law in bringing Russia to realize its fullest potential. It will be surprising if he really seeks to emulate the style of Chile's former military dictator, Augusto Pinochet, despite his early rumblings to that effect. With respect to the virtues of checks and balances as norms of governance for which to strive, his party's platform, for the most part, has genuflected in the proper direction.

Lebed seems determined to go head-to-head with the Russian mafia. He recently announced that he has negotiated an agreement with Moscow's mayor, Yury Luzhkov, to field-test an anticrime strategy first in Moscow and the Moscow region. "Then we will see," he said, "who is stronger—the Moscow Internal Affairs department or the local rogues."[7] If he tries to take on the crime tarbaby in earnest, however, it could devour him or, worse yet, make him a laughingstock for being ineffective. Peter Reddaway has predicted that Lebed will launch a frontal attack on corruption and organized crime, but that these forces in the end "will almost certainly defeat him."[8] Be that as it may, Lebed faces a tall order indeed in any attempt to wrestle to the ground singlehandedly what is perhaps Russia's most overbearing social problem today.

As for the continuing unpleasantness in Chechnya, Lebed is, at this writing, working overtime to end the confrontation as soon as possible, remove all Russian occupation forces, evacuate any Russian minorities desirous of leaving, and lock up a negotiated settlement that precludes any resurgence of fighting (see the next chapter for further discussion). He takes seriously the explosive potential that lurks in continued Russian combat involvement against the Chechen resistance and has stated his belief that such turbulence, left unchecked, could spark a civil war, something he is determined to

---

[6]Georgie Anne Geyer, "Enlightening Visit with Russia's General Lebed," *Washington Times*, October 31, 1995.

[7]Mayak Radio Network, Moscow, June 27, 1996.

[8]Peter Reddaway, "Russia Heads for Trouble," *New York Times*, July 2, 1996.

prevent. As in the case of his promises to resolve the crime and corruption issue, it remains to be seen whether Lebed can match his rhetoric on Chechnya with a lasting solution.

The Security Council under Lebed's tutelage will almost certainly play a more influential role than before in Russia's defense and security policymaking, if only because of the power and magnetism of Lebed's personality. Shortly after Yeltsin's victory, Lebed announced that new leaders in the Ministry of Defense, the Federal Security Services (FSB), and other security-related agencies "will bring fresh blood and minds to the common cause." He further declared that "good ideas will not remain just on paper. I promise this."[9] In a clear move aimed at broadening his base of technical expertise, Lebed recently hired as his deputy, with Yeltsin's approval, Dr. Nikolai Mikhailov, an experienced defense-sector engineer and senior manager who previously was president of the interstate corporation *Vympel* ("Banner"), a major scientific research enterprise concerned with, among other things, high-technology ballistic missile defense applications.[10]

According to Yury Baturin, who preceded Lebed as Yeltsin's Security Council secretary, that position has now been combined with the post of Presidential Assistant for National Security in what Baturin termed "a logical step" which had "suggested itself for a long time" and with which he was personally content, "even if it came at the cost of my removal."[11] The prospect of Lebed's Security Council becoming a bureaucratic juggernaut, however, should not be overstated. The Russian security policy apparatus remains poorly institutionalized, and personal rivals can be counted on to build alliances and form counterbalances. In particular, Lebed has stated his belief that the FSB, including its counterintelligence units, is "much weakened, inefficient and practically disabled." He has called for a return of competent professionals to this system and for efforts to "improve coordination among security departments." He ducked a question as to whether there should be a merger of the FSB, the

---

[9]Mayak Radio Network, Moscow, July 4, 1996.

[10]Interfax, Moscow, July 29, 1996.

[11]Interview with Baturin by Leonid Nikitinskii, "Yury Baturin Hands Over Matters and Backs Up His Successor." *Moskovskiye novosti*, June 25–30, 1996.

Border Guards, and the Federal Agency for Government Communications and Information, allowing only that any consideration of forming a central intelligence service (essentially a recreation of a unitary KGB) to coordinate all foreign intelligence activity would have to await political decisions, financing, and personnel appointments. He said that there were many options and that the challenge was to pick the most sensible one.[12]

Clearly, Lebed is seeking a broadened mandate for the Security Council. He once noted, in the course of reorganizing the Council's functions, that his analysts would be looking for useful lessons drawn from the experience of other countries with institutions that fulfill similar roles.[13] He has also stated that by its new draft charter, the Security Council will concern itself with the four areas of national defense, public safety, economic security, and information security, and that it will consist of four directorates tasked with day-to-day responsibility for these areas.[14] This all plays to Lebed's long-range political goals. But it also puts him on a potential collision course with others in the administration, notably Chubais, Chernomyrdin, and, ultimately, perhaps Yeltsin himself. Working to his advantage in this respect, however, at least on paper, is Lebed's statutory right to report directly to the president, under whom his office was directly subordinated by a decree signed by Yeltsin on July 10.[15]

By virtue of his background and upbringing, military reform is Lebed's strongest suit, as well as the policy issue on which his public statements have been most detailed and in which he has the greatest chance of making real progress over the long term. His Security Council charter now puts him in charge of policy planning, and he is answered to in this respect by the defense minister and the chief of the General Staff as well as by the service chiefs.[16] It is doubtful that

---

[12]Interfax, Moscow, July 2, 1996.

[13]Viktoriya Likhovtseva, "The Security Council Will Take On Restoring Order in the Economy," *Finansoviye izvestiia*, June 27, 1996.

[14]Russian Public Television First Channel Network, Moscow, July 11, 1996.

[15]"Yeltsin Decrees Lebed Directly Subordinated to President." ITAR-TASS, Moscow, July 11, 1996.

[16]"Presidential Bulletin" feature, Interfax, Moscow, June 21, 1996.

he will be seriously challenged in this important role. At all levels, the Russian military has long awaited an honest and incorruptible leader to raise morale and return the institution to good health. They now have one in Lebed. Accordingly, they will be inclined to give him not just the benefit of the doubt, but their strong support. This could prove to be a mixed blessing for the West, however, should Russian-American relations take a serious turn for the worst.

Where personnel matters are concerned, Lebed has avowed that important leadership posts will no longer be filled by "good old boys," but rather by professionals who can meet the objective test of competence. He added that a sizable number of young generals, colonels, and lieutenant colonels discharged by Grachev for standing on principle remain valued assets to the cause of reform, and that his inclination is to return them to duty, since "the country needs them."[17] He further stated that people like the recently dismissed chief of defense finance Lieutenant General Vasily Vorobyev had discredited the profession by their bad example, and he vowed to deal uncompromisingly with corruption and embezzlement within the ranks. In attesting to his own purity of motive on this score, he averred that had he taken the darker path that beckoned seductively while he was 14th Army commander, "carrying out all the stupid orders of the defense ministry" while selling off weapons for personal gain, he would "have everything today: a high post in the Ministry of Defense, millions of dollars in foreign banks, and villas not only in the nearby Moscow suburbs, but also in the more desirable places around the world."[18]

Regarding his promise to end the epidemic of corruption in the military, Lebed has struck a responsive chord. There has already been expectant talk at the working level in the defense ministry of the impending creation of something like a "waste, fraud and abuse" hotline prompted by his arrival as the new sheriff in town. One reporter noted that Lebed is widely seen in the ministry as "a kind of idol" and a "god bringing hope." He predicted that there would soon be "a line

---

[17]Interview by Igor Korotchenko, "Everybody Needs a Secure Russia," *Nezavisimaia gazeta*, June 22, 1991.

[18]Interview by Aleksandr Zhilin, "'I Am Not a Political Killer. . .' A First-Hand Account," *Moskovskiye novosti*, June 25–30, 1996.

of people wanting to give him a list of the injustices and illegalities committed by senior defense ministry officers and generals." He added that the ministry's computer network had already begun working for Lebed, with dozens of "enthusiasts now storing data on who stole what, when, where, and how much; who grabbed an apartment with defense ministry money; who privatized a dacha; who pushed through a consignment of weapons; and so on."[19]

Lebed may also try, as his KRO party platform proposed, to depoliticize the military through legislation. Beyond that, he can be expected to push to end draft exemptions for sons of the well-to-do and to crack down hard on draft evasion—on the premise that conscription must gather the best of Russia's youth, since an all-volunteer military entails costs beyond Russia's reach. He has voiced deep doubts about the feasibility of Yeltsin's campaign promise to end the draft and create a professional military before the year 2000. This could lead to friction with the president if it proceeds beyond the talking stage. During the campaign, Lebed argued, on good ground, that Yeltsin's easy promise to convert the military into an all-volunteer force was infeasible because of its excessive cost. As he bluntly remarked, "someone either stupid or very devious put the president up to that idea.[20] Short of ending the draft, however, Lebed seems determined to eliminate the more blatant abuses of the existing system, notably the brutal hazing (known as *dedovshchina)* of first-year inductees by older conscripts. Shortly before the July 3 runoff, he gave vent to apparently genuine hurt feelings that people were trying to show him to be a "monster." He countered that he merely wants to turn Russia's military into a healthy and proper one, "which will be our pride and which will not be frightening for mothers whose sons are being called up."[21]

---

[19]Igor Chernyak, "Generals Will Be Fired in Platoons," *Komsomolskaia pravda*, July 2, 1996.

[20]Quoted in Valery Begishev, "A Union of Two Politicians," *Lesnaia gazeta*, June 25, 1996. Yeltsin's new defense minister, Colonel General Igor Rodionov, voiced his own reservations rather more discreetly, stating that shifting over to an all-volunteer army involves "a very complex task" which will be feasible only if, "first and foremost, the economic preconditions are put into place to establish an armed forces of this type." Interview on Russian Television Network, Moscow, July 28, 1996.

[21]Russian Public Television Network, Moscow, July 1, 1996.

Lebed announced that he has specific plans for reforming the military, but that he will not disclose these until they are first ratified by Yeltsin. He also evidently has plans for the Ministry of Defense. He recently commented that the defense minister is really no more than a minister of the five armed services and that this purview "has no relation to the larger part of the uniformed ranks [i.e., other arms like the Ministry of Internal Affairs and FSB] and I think this is wrong. All of those who bear arms must know exactly where they stand in the country's defense system. So in peacetime, let them function as independently as they will, but there must be a system capable of taking firm control of the whole of the armed forces. This is what I intend to build."[22] He added that the military badly needs to get rid of its many separate internal baronies and vertical reporting chains, citing as a case in point how Russia's forces in Chechnya "always have to fight as individual units, like fingers, and these fingers are always being broken." To fix this problem, he said, "the system must clench itself into a fist"—Lebed's metaphor for integration and jointness.[23] He repeated his firm belief that the debacle in Chechnya was due partly to a compartmented military organizational structure at all levels, which caused the right hand all too often not to know what the left was doing.

Included in what is known thus far about Lebed's military reform ideas is the elimination of skeleton divisions. "If one takes a map of Russia today and puts the headquarters of all divisions and brigades and shows it to someone," he recently pointed out, "it will seem to him that it is a monster of a country! Look how many divisions, how many brigades it has!"[24] Correcting this problem, he declared, will not require any new investment. The military's organization will simply be trimmed down. In connection with this declared plan, Lebed said that he will propose to Yeltsin that the latter should announce that the military in 1997–1998 will abandon its current practice of maintaining undermanned units, with those having only 25–30 percent of the required manning level being turned into storage bases.

---

[22]Interview on Radio Station *Ekho Moskvy*, June 20, 1996.

[23]Russian Public Television Network, Moscow, July 1, 1996.

[24]Comment on "Vote or Lose" program, Fifth Channel Television Network, St. Petersburg, June 21, 1996.

Lebed has promised to reduce the Russian armed forces by a third. As a case in point, he said that fifteen fully manned and combat-ready divisions are better than 100 undermanned ones. He has called for a new three-tiered army structure consisting of airborne forces and specially trained general-purpose units at level one, fully manned infantry and armored formations with appropriate equipment and munitions at level two, and bases, storage facilities, and logistic structures at level three. Such "small mobile fists," he said, "can solve all problems."[25]

Lebed will probably stick with the existing Russian five-service arrangement at least for the time being, if his party platform is any guide. He will also probably pursue reform measures that focus on building a healthy military institution before seeking to acquire new hardware for its own sake. At the same time he will press hard, in the face of Russia's continuing cash shortage, for increased allocations to defense. He will also strive to resurrect the military industry.

With respect to the latter, Lebed has proposed a long-term program of retraining military and industry specialists, reducing the tax burden on enterprises of the defense industry so as to stimulate their incentives to produce, repaying state debts to industry, fully financing alternative production programs for defense industry capacity that has become surplus, and restoring Russia's position in the global arms market.[26] A problem with at least part of this approach is that it calls for an expensive bailout of inefficient or unneeded production facilities that instead should be allowed to die.

Finally, Lebed has declared his intent to deal forthrightly with the chronic nonpayment of salaries to military personnel and the insufficiency of food, clothing, fuel and oil, and other essential consumables. To help correct these deficiencies, he has proposed that procurement orders issued by the concerned ministries be supplied at cost, without the obligation to subsidize the suppliers' tax liability. He complained that escalating tax increases have made goods for the military twice as expensive as they need to be.

---

[25]Interfax, Moscow, July 2, 1996.

[26]Comment on Moscow NTV, July 2, 1996.

The pro-reform *Moskovskii komsomolets* has suggested that Lebed may not have as easy a time with military reform as it might appear at first glance, since his contacts in some service branches are limited and since he seems to be having trouble putting together a team of trusted subordinates.[27] Nevertheless, Lebed knows the Russian military well. Unlike his predecessor, he will work hard to reinvest it with a sense of pride and professionalism. He is one of the few people who the ranks believe could actually carry out serious reform rather than merely mouth the right words. Moscow defense correspondent Pavel Felgengauer hit the nail on the head when he wrote that on the question of what needs fixing in the military, "Lebed's views are mature and settled. At long last, Yeltsin has a person in high office who understands the problems of the military. Lebed's appointment creates the possibility that the Russian army will reform, rather than just mutiny."[28]

As far as Russia's security interests abroad are concerned, Lebed will not be inclined to sign on to gratuitously assertive international stances, if only because of his appreciation of Russia's weakened international power position. He is not spoiling for trouble, and he sees the country's problems as falling mainly on the home front. With such an outlook, perhaps he can even be a stabilizing influence if he grows into his assignment and gains real effectiveness as an insider rather than an outsider.

EXTERNAL CONCERNS

Internationally, Lebed can be expected to leave his mark primarily in three areas: (1) Russia's security strategy, (2) the disposition of tensions in the so-called "near abroad," and (3) Russia's response to NATO enlargement.

On the first account, Lebed has announced that the conceptual framework for a new Russian approach to security already exists and that the challenge is to establish a mechanism for its implementa-

---

[27]Cited in Michael R. Gordon, "Yeltsin, in Another Political Purge, Dismisses 7 Top Generals," *New York Times*, June 26, 1996.

[28]Quoted in Vanora Bennett, "New No. 2 Man in Russia Faces Uncertain Future," *Los Angeles Times*, June 30, 1996.

tion.[29] Still, the odds are scant that he will seek to pursue an expansionist policy beyond the borders of the former Soviet Union. More than any other nationalist contender for president, he understands that Russia lacks the wherewithal to pursue such a strategy, even were it deemed to be attractive in principle. In his outlook on Russia's place in the world, he seems to bear out James Billington's view that Americans need not reflexively assume that the Russians "have some genetic predisposition to produce another threatening form of nationalism." He likewise offers a plausible fit with Billington's suggestion that "a more positive Russian nationalism compatible with democracy seems more likely to prevail."[30] Lebed's main concern is that Russia regain its self-respect and be taken seriously in the major capitals around the world. He has cited Russia's marginalization in the Yugoslav crisis as a classic illustration of what can happen when a once-great power loses its former clout.

Lebed freely admits that the USSR lost the cold war because of the bankrupt policies of the communists. Accordingly, he will not be inclined to seek any settling of old scores with the United States and NATO. Although fiercely independent and self-assured in his own way, he will almost certainly eschew the far-out visions of Zhirinovsky. Lebed is not a jingoist, and he has taken a decided stance against organizations that support fascism. He can be expected, however, to take a strong lead in nurturing the development and articulation of a security concept for Russia that will reassert Russia's status as a global power short of confrontation with the West. As he declared emphatically after the June presidential election, "those who believe in me must have no doubts: Russia will reemerge as a great power."[31]

As for the "near abroad," Lebed feels strong compulsions to honor the social and political protection needs of the 25 million Russians living in the former Soviet republics. It is unlikely, however, that he will advocate outright coercion toward that end or pursue lesser

---

[29]Dispatch by Andrei Surzhanskii and Mikhail Shevstsov, ITAR-TASS, Moscow, June 27, 1996.

[30]James H. Billington, "Let Russia Be Russian," *New York Times*, June 16, 1996.

[31]Interview by Igor Korotchenko, "Everybody Needs a Secure Russia," *Nezavisimaia gazeta*, June 22, 1991.

means that blatantly violate the sovereignty of the newly independent states. There was little closeness, it should be noticed, between Lebed and the corrupt leadership of the rump Russian Transdniester Republic in Moldova. As 14th Army commander, Lebed's sole concern was to protect the rights of Russians living in a foreign land, not the interests of an illegitimate regime harboring self-delusional political fantasies. Lebed has admitted that economic integration out of mutual self-interest and a possible confederation among consenting former republics constitute the outer limits of any acceptable Russian effort to put Humpty Dumpty back together again.

Lebed can be expected, however, to argue for firm steps against any eastward expansion of NATO that does not expressly make a satisfactory offsetting provision for Russia's security concerns and sense of being first among equals in Central Europe. This should come as no surprise to anyone in the West. Lebed's earlier declared views on NATO enlargement were more blustery in the articulation than many. But at bottom, his perspective on the issue has been quintessentially mainstream. Lebed has expressed special concern about Germany's potential for resurgence at Russia's expense. He will no doubt pursue a strategy aimed at containing any German ambition for a return to dominance in Europe should Russia become squeezed, without compensation, by a NATO that moves ever closer toward its western edge.

Lebed has voiced skepticism over Partnership for Peace, NATO's arrangement for engaging the military establishments of the former Warsaw Pact states, including Russia. This may reflect merely his underdeveloped worldliness owing to his little first-hand exposure to the West. Insofar as it is a real problem, it should be remediable by astute American and NATO initiatives aimed at engaging him constructively. One concern that might incline Lebed to think especially hard about the merits of a cooperative security relationship with the West is his evident unease over China's ambitions and long-term strategic prospects.

Chapter Nine

LEBED'S NEAR-TERM POLITICAL PROSPECTS

So much for Lebed's avowed policy inclinations. A matter of greater import is how successful he will be in following through on them. Can Lebed deliver in the Moscow political environment? One might recall here Harry Truman's comment to similar effect about Dwight Eisenhower when the former five-star general was leading in the polls against Adlai Stevenson in 1952. "No professional general," said Truman, "has ever made a good president. The art of war is too different from the art of civilian government." Later, after Eisenhower's election victory, Truman mused aloud in an exchange with several staffers in the Oval Office: "He'll sit right here and he'll say do this, do that! And nothing will happen. Poor Ike—it won't be a bit like the Army. He'll find it very frustrating."[1] To say the least, Lebed's background as a field commander has not prepared him well for his new role as a Kremlin politician. Some predict that with his narrow military upbringing, his general officer's mindset, and his unsophisticated ways for the complex world he now occupies, he will eventually suffer a political downfall akin to that of former Soviet air force general and Afghan War hero Aleksandr Rutskoi three years before.

There is also Lebed's rich history of insubordination, which raises doubts whether he will be any more controllable by Yeltsin as an insider than he was by Grachev as an outsider. Indeed, his own pronouncements of late have given good ground to believe that he will

---

[1]Quoted in David McCullough, *Truman*, New York, Simon and Schuster, 1992, pp. 912–914.

continue to march to his own drummer and will be difficult to manage at best. The critical issue here is whether Lebed will have the flexibility to operate effectively in a world quite unlike the one to which he has become accustomed throughout his career to date.

A PERSONA IN FLUX?

Clearly, Lebed tends to take a Manichaean view of the world, dividing it into forces of good and evil without much shading in between. Two months before his appointment as Yeltsin's security adviser, a former CIA expert in psychiatric profiles of major international figures wrote that the retired general is "decisive but inflexible" and has a black-and-white mentality which has shown difficulty coping with ambiguity, the idea of compromise, and being willing to negotiate.[2]

Nonetheless, Lebed has not remained mired in rigid habit patterns of the past. On the contrary, he has worked hard, and with some success, to polish his skills as a politician. His seeming retrenchment on NATO enlargement offers one promising sign that he may be acquiring a more pragmatic policy outlook. Much the same can be said of his acceptance of the desirability of a smaller and more professional military. (Earlier, he had insisted that this would not be acceptable.) Such shifts raise a question about the extent to which one can gauge his future behavior from things he has said in the past.

Lebed insists that he is not a conniver. This is probably an honest self-assessment. It is also significant, for his very guilelessness could contribute to his undoing, if he does not learn how to take care of himself in the cutthroat world of Moscow intrigue.

Lebed also admits that his instinct is to rise above the fray: "I am absolutely free of megalomania and, in general, am not seeking a quarrel with anybody. . . . I am not a petty or malicious person. I have never settled scores with anyone and have no intention of starting now."[3] That last comment, however, transcends disingenuousness if

---

[2]See Anthony Pridotkas and Jerrold M. Post, M.D., "Aleksandr Lebed, In Defense of the Motherland," *Post-Soviet Prospects*, Washington, D.C., Center for Strategic and International Studies, No. 5, April 1996.

[3]Interview on "Hero of the Day" program, Moscow NTV, June 18, 1996.

one considers Lebed's long-simmering relationship with Grachev, the recent dismissal of whom was one of Russia's more spectacular settling of old scores in recent times by any measure. Of the dismissal, Lebed said frankly in a different context that it was "overdue," since Grachev "had allowed the military to vegetate under inhumane conditions," and that he [Lebed] was "unable to watch that any longer."[4]

It remains to be seen whether Lebed will be able to abide for long the petty humiliations and daily hassles that are the lot of a bureaucratic politician. As an army general, he had grown accustomed to having things his way. He will need to develop new expectations and habit patterns if he is to succeed in his new incarnation. Indeed, he has already shown at least once that he is not above throwing his weight around with the inner circle of handlers surrounding the president. By one account, Lebed requested an appointment with Yeltsin on the election runoff day of July 3 and was curtly told by Yeltsin's aide, Viktor Ilyushin, that such a meeting was out of the question. Lebed reportedly went ballistic and threatened the president's assistant that if he could not see Yeltsin, he would drive straight to CNN and "tell the world that Boris Nikolayevich is dead." He got his requested meeting.[5]

Moreover, as unseasoned as Lebed still may be in the game of Kremlin intrigue, he is scarcely clueless with regard to the machinations now taking place around him. After Chernomyrdin aggressively insisted that he was taking charge of the investigation into two closely spaced incidents in which bombs destroyed two Moscow trolleys two days in a row, only hours after Yeltsin had signed a decree granting Lebed wide and uncontested powers to fight crime and corruption, a senior Lebed aide remarked laconically: "We got the point of it. We're not stupid. But you know, if he [Chernomyrdin] is going to spend all year trying to do Lebed's job, then Mr. Chubais will be able to spend all year controlling the economy."[6]

---

[4]Quoted in "To Establish Order" *Der Spiegel* (Hamburg), June 24, 1996, pp. 129–131.

[5]David Remnick, "The War for the Kremlin," *The New Yorker*, July 22, 1996, p. 57.

[6]Michael Specter, "Yeltsin's New Kremlin," *New York Times*, July 18, 1996.

On the positive side, Lebed could serve as a moderating counter-weight to the tendency of Yevgeny Primakov's foreign ministry to cozy up to troublesome countries like China and Iran. Already, Lebed may have tried to paper over a minor contretemps with Japan when he conceded the existence of a legitimate territorial dispute over the Kuril Islands and stressed that any resolution will require "a thorough analysis of all proposals, including an analysis of the understanding of the problem on the Japanese side."[7] Earlier, Primakov had said peremptorily that any resolution should be left to future generations, prompting an angry Japanese reply that it had to be resolved now. (Also earlier, while he was still 14th Army commander in Moldova, Lebed himself had expressed a far more intemperate nationalist outlook on the touchy issue of the Kurils.)

If Lebed can control his ambitions, remain directed and focused, and play to his greatest professional strengths, he has every chance of gaining credibility as a politician and building a foundation for bigger things to come. This will mean, however, concentrating on those issues where he can make a real difference and not squandering his energy in needless Kremlin turf wars.

INVITATIONS TO TROUBLE

Lebed has spoken injudiciously on several occasions since his ascent to power and, in the process, has shown a darker side of his personality, at least in the eyes of those already inclined to fear or distrust him. His recurrent outbursts and other verbal indiscretions in the short span of time between the election and the runoff prompted many observers who were initially inclined to give him the benefit of the doubt to chalk him up as a "loose cannon."[8] For example, perhaps more out of indiscipline than real conviction, he lashed out at what he called the West's "cultural expansion," as evidenced by the dominance of Western movies on Russian television. He insisted

---

[7]Dispatch by Andrei Surzhanskii and Andrei Varlamov, ITAR-TASS, Moscow, June 27, 1996.

[8]See, for example, "Russia Buries the Past," *Wall Street Journal*, July 5, 1996. This commentary added that Lebed was coming across unabashedly as a nationalist, protectionist, and authoritarian figure, and declared that "quite possibly the wisest thing Mr. Yeltsin could do would be to shove him aside after some decent interval."

that countering this corrupting influence on Russian values would constitutes one of the cornerstones of his national security policy.[9]

Lebed further charged that alien religions like Japan's Aum Shinrikyo sect "corrupt the people and ruin the state" and "must be outlawed," on the ground that they represent a "direct threat to national security." He said that Russia has three "officially recognized" religions—the Orthodox Church, Islam, and Buddhism—while conspicuously omitting Judaism, even though the latter is commonly viewed in Russia as a nationality as much as a faith. Before the July 3 runoff, he added that Russia should tighten its entry requirements for foreigners and ban some religious groups outright, including the Mormon Church, as designated threats to the state. He called these churches "mold and scum" brought into the country "with the purpose of perverting, corrupting, and breaking up our state."[10] Responding to the meek and apologetic tone of one supportive questioner at a rally, he shot back: "You say you're a Cossack. Why do you speak like a Jew?"[11] He later apologized once the intensity and depth of international reaction to these crude pronouncements were brought home to him.

Topping these gaffes showing religious and cultural intolerance has been an unseemly overreaching by Lebed to seek a hand in decisionmaking on the economy and foreign investment, as well as an aggressive quest on his part for a truly wall-to-wall definition of "security." On both accounts, the London *Economist* took him to task for his "ugly, economically illiterate, and antidemocratic remarks" since the election, pronouncing that they "confirm suspicions that he is the wrong man for the succession."[12] It later slammed what it derisively termed these "antics" of Yeltsin's "boisterous new national security adviser and would-be dauphin."[13]

---

[9]Dispatch by Mikhail Shevstsov and Andrei Surzhanskii, ITAR-TASS, Moscow, June 27, 1996.

[10]Quoted in Richard Boudreaux, "Yeltsin Aide Denounces Foreigners, Urges Curbs," *Los Angeles Times*, June 28, 1996.

[11]Quoted in Alessandra Stanley, "For Yeltsin's New Kremlin Team, Chickens Come Home to Roost," *New York Times*, June 28, 1996.

[12]"Yeltsin's Next Round," *The Economist* (London), July 6, 1996, p. 17.

[13]"Normal Intrigue," *The Economist* (London), July 13, 1996, p. 46.

Clearly Lebed was asking for trouble when he claimed that his security mandate included such questionable matters as safeguarding Russia's food supply, regulating the country's banking, and overseeing privatization, the use of state funds, regional policy, the transport infrastructure, foreign trade, and currency control.[14]

Perhaps most consequential for Lebed over the longer haul may be the extent of his own political ambition and his less than whole-hearted obeisance to his most pivotal benefactor to date, President Yeltsin. Lebed's loyalty to Yeltsin remains decidedly thin. Responding earlier to a campaign worker who asked whether he would be meeting with voters in the south of Russia on Yeltsin's behalf, he replied: "I'm a general, not a dancer."[15] Asked whether he saw himself as Russia's next president after Yeltsin's second term expires in 2000, Lebed replied "possibly sooner," in an almost breathtakingly indiscreet reference to the president's shaky health.[16] Lebed told a German newsweekly that his current role in the Yeltsin government is only an "intermediate" step in his still-unfolding political career.[17]

A month before the June election, Lebed also refused to cooperate with those urging him to join hands with Fyodorov and Yavlinsky in withdrawing their collective candidacies in return for a suitable plum from the president. Lebed stated that he could not accept such an entreaty for the "simple reason that the current authorities are no better than the communists. I am convinced that as long as the nomenklatura is running this country—whether with party cards or tricolor flags—there will be no normal life. Both the 'Whites' and the 'Reds' are united in one thing—they are birds from the same nomenklatura nest. But I'm from a different nest."[18]

Lebed refused to go on the stump for Yeltsin on the proclaimed ground that he is no "organizer of mass public entertainment." He

[14]Viktoriya Likhovtseva, "The Security Council Will Take On Restoring Order in the Economy," *Finansoviye izvestiia*, June 27, 1996.

[15]Quoted in Stanley, *New York Times*, June 28, 1996.

[16]Quoted in Michael R. Gordon, "Russian Vote Sets Off Battle, This Time in Yeltsin's Camp," *New York Times*, July 6, 1996.

[17]*Der Spiegel* (Hamburg), June 24, 1996, pp. 129–131.

[18]Vasily Kononenko, "Lebed Not Planning to Join Democratic Coalition," *Izvestiia*, May 13, 1996.

said that he planned to remain fully preoccupied with Security Council matters throughout the remainder of the campaign.[19] He further staunchly refused to endorse Yeltsin's candidacy even *after* the president had brought him on board as security adviser, insisting that he is "not a trader" and "cannot be bought."[20] Right up to the July 3 runoff, Lebed remained studiously neutral when it came to pressures for him to endorse the Russian president and swing his constituency to Yeltsin's support. Indeed, he went so far once as to take a direct swipe at the hand that was feeding him. Lumping the finalists together, Lebed said that he had good reason to consider both as being "far from ideal leaders for such a complex country as Russia," and that he would "not campaign either for Yeltsin or Zyuganov."[21] After what Yeltsin had offered him, the latter would have had every reason to regard this high-handed posturing of Lebed's as an ungrateful affront.

As one Russian commentator suggested, it may be only a matter of time before "the general battling evil in the Russian leadership will find himself in the position of the sergeant-major who is out of step with his company."[22] Some maintain that in handing him the law-and-order portfolio, Yeltsin may intentionally have given Lebed a political time bomb as a tacit payback for his overly exuberant independence. Others are convinced that this thankless assignment is Mission Impossible and that it will eventually consume Lebed despite his best efforts. There could even be physical dangers, although direct threats from the underworld have not yet been levied against Lebed, at least publicly.[23] In all events, Lebed has yet to demonstrate by his political comportment since joining the Yeltsin team that he

---

[19]Dispatch by Andrei Shtorkh, ITAR-TASS World Service, Moscow, June 18, 1996.

[20]Interview on NTV, Moscow, June 18, 1996.

[21]Quoted in Yury Karash and Martin Sieff, "Lebed Remains Neutral for Runoff," *Washington Times*, June 20, 1996.

[22]Vladimir Shelkov, "Even the United States Is Praising the Russian President for Giving an Important Job to a Once Out-of-Favor General," *Pravda*, June 21–28, 1996.

[23]Notably, however, Lebed is scarcely unmindful of the personal risks created by his aggressive and high-profile stances on a number of threatening fronts. He recently told a British reporter: "I could be blown up by a bomb, I could be killed by a bullet. The main thing, first of all, is to survive." Quoted in an interview by Chrystia Freeland, *Financial Times* (London), July 25, 1996.

will not, in the end, prove to be his own worst enemy as his career continues to unfold.

THE RESURGENCE IN CHECHNYA AND ITS PORTENTS

If Lebed was headed for a showdown sooner or later with his political enemies in Moscow, the massive attack launched by Chechen rebels on August 6, 1996, to retake Grozny neatly conspired to make it sooner. Until that unexpected initiative forced Lebed's hand, he had vacillated on what to do about Chechnya, not only by retracting his earlier strong commitment to a referendum on Chechen independence, but also by equivocating on when he would undertake his long-promised trip for an on-scene look at how best to resolve the crisis. Indeed, only the weekend before, perhaps in line with his determination to adopt a lower profile amid all the Kremlin intrigue, he declared that he had abandoned his initial plans for an early visit to Chechnya. Western observers speculated that this new posture reflected either powerlessness or a change of heart on Lebed's part.[24]

The first day after the rebel assault, however, Lebed revealed his intent to seek a negotiated settlement rather than to escalate the fighting when, after duly underscoring the "guilt" of the Chechen resistance for inflicting the bloodshed in the first place, he declared that the Security Council did not plan to solve the new crisis "exclusively by coercive means." He added that the Council was working toward convening a congress of Chechens of all persuasions, with the objective of laying "a sound foundation for a wide discussion of peace alternatives to solve the problem instead of an atmosphere of exhaustion and bitterness."[25] Of course, Lebed was quick to point out that, absent a rebel willingness to end the fighting, Russian forces would do what they had to do to protect themselves. Clearly, however, he was seizing this moment in a spirit of conciliation.

Prime Minister Chernomyrdin concurred that a negotiated outcome offered the only acceptable way to end the war. He conspicuously

---

[24]See, for example, James Rupert, "Chechen Rebels Assault Grozny as Yeltsin Returns to Moscow," *Washington Post*, August 7, 1996.

[25]Interfax, Moscow, August 7, 1996.

ducked any personal responsibility for bringing such a settlement to fruition, however, tossing that hot potato squarely to Lebed: "Lebed is a military man, and he is more qualified to deal with such problems." Characteristically, though, on the heels of his declaration of belief that Lebed "will and must cope with this task," he indicated, through a spokesman, that any future trips by Lebed to the war zone "had not been approved."[26]

The next day, however, Lebed set off on the first of what were to be three trips to Chechnya in the space of two weeks for meetings with the rebel commander, General Aslan Maskhadov. Earlier, some of Yeltsin's aides had carped from the sidelines over Lebed's seeming refusal to make good on his campaign promise to travel to Chechnya. This mission was aimed in part at putting an end to such gratuitous potshots. Almost immediately, Lebed's arrival in Grozny prompted a tone of respectful optimism from the rebel leaders, suggesting that if any Russian could make a difference, it was he. Said the rebel spokesman Movladi Udugov, "if General Lebed fulfills his electoral promises to end the war, we will do all we can so that Russian state interests are preserved in the Caucasus and Chechnya and Russians get out of this war while saving face."[27]

This first visit by Lebed to Chechnya yielded the initial outlines of a cease-fire plan, described by Lebed as Yeltsin-approved, which would convene a congress of interested Chechens to replace the Moscow-appointed puppet government and to select an assembly that would rewrite the Chechen constitution—possibly to include a provision for limited Chechen autonomy within the Russian Federation. At a Moscow press conference upon his return, Lebed had words of respect for the rebel forces, calling them "good fighters" and "fine soldiers" and contrasting them starkly to Russia's own pathetic troops, which he said he was shocked to discover were "hungry, lice-ridden, and half-clothed creatures" overwhelmed by logistic and morale problems.[28] He suggested that Russian partisan guerrillas in

---

[26]Vanora Bennett, "Russian Lawmakers Reelect Prime Minister," *Los Angeles Times*, August 11, 1996.

[27]Quoted in Michael Specter, "Russians Failing to Wrest Grozny from Insurgents," *New York Times*, August 12, 1996.

[28]Richard Boudreaux and Vanora Bennett, "Secret Visit to Chechnya Produces Plan for Peace," *Los Angeles Times*, August 13, 1996.

World War II had been better clothed and that these deprived soldiers should be removed from the combat zone for "purely humanitarian reasons."[29]

Directing his anger at those in Moscow whom he saw as responsible for perpetrating this tragedy, Lebed then fired a broadside at the "passivity" and "corruption" of those officials who had been charged with achieving a resolution of the crisis, pointing out in particular that the commission headed by Chernomyrdin had "failed." As for his sudden selection by Yeltsin to replace Oleg Lobov as Russia's envoy to Chechnya, with full responsibility for that portfolio and all the high-profile risk that went with it, Lebed declared: "This shows that someone wants me very much to break my neck over this assignment. We shall see. I like tough assignments. They excite me." Lebed added his belief that the appointment was a product of bureaucratic intrigue, said that it had been made without his knowledge or consent, and indicated that he had first learned of it from his secretary. He went on to say that the rebels had agreed to talks on a truce and that he gave such talks a "90-percent chance" of success.[30]

The decree by Yeltsin granting Lebed broad powers to end the war was said to authorize the latter to "coordinate the activities" of the various federal agencies involved, presumably including the defense and internal-affairs ministries. It also dissolved the earlier commission headed by Chernomyrdin, which Lebed had criticized as being ineffective.[31] Initially, this seemed to have been a tactical victory for Lebed. A setback came, however, when Lebed returned to Grozny a second time on August 15, only to learn that he had a major problem of insubordination in the acting Russian commander, Lieutenant General Konstantin Pulikovskii.

Although Yeltsin had endorsed Lebed's draft blueprint for a long-term settlement upon the latter's return to Moscow from his previous trip, Pulikovskii's subsequent cessation of talks with the rebels

---

[29]Alessandra Stanley, "Yeltsin Security Aide Denounces Russian Conduct Over Chechnya," *New York Times*, August 13, 1996.

[30]Lee Hockstader, "Lebed Explores Truce With Chechen Rebels," *Washington Post*, August 13, 1996.

[31]Lee Hockstader, "Yeltsin Gives Lebed Wide Powers to End Chechen War," *Washington Post*, August 15, 1996.

and his resumption of combat operations when the rebel side insisted on full independence indicated at least passive resistance to Lebed's initiative within parts of the Russian military.[32] For his part, Lebed indicated that he saw "the sincere intention of the president to do all that is possible to stop this war" and that this was why he [Lebed] had been given "sufficient powers to deal with this problem." However, he compared the Kremlin intrigue to "swimming in hydrochloric acid with your legs cut off." It was reported that Anatoly Chubais was the one who had objected to Yeltsin's granting Lebed plenipotentiary powers in Chechnya, on the ground that they played to Lebed's personal ambitions.

As for Pulikovskii's resistance to implementing a cease-fire, Lebed summoned the Russian generals assigned to the war zone for a private caucus and emerged to tell reporters that the confrontation was being dragged on for "commercial reasons."[33] Upon returning to Moscow the following day, he said angrily of Russia's continued embroilment in Chechnya that "a pauper country with a doddering economy and army cannot afford the luxury of fighting a war." He then pulled out all the stops, zeroing in on the hard-line Minister of Internal Affairs, Colonel General Anatoly Kulikov, and branding him "one of the main culprits in the Chechen tragedy." Handing Yeltsin a point-blank ultimatum, he declared: "You have a hard choice— either Lebed or Kulikov."[34]

Not to be cowed, Kulikov snapped back that such "slander and insults" from Lebed attested to the latter's "maniacal desire for power." Kulikov, whose troops had done much of the day-to-day fighting in Chechnya since the initial invasion in December 1994, had taken to speaking contemptuously of the peace process and to scorning the rebels as "medieval savages" who cannot be trusted. In defending himself against Lebed's charge, he added that the recent recapture of Grozny by rebel forces was not the result of any mistakes by his min-

---

[32]Vanora Bennett, "Chechnya 'Truce' Starts With Russian Bomb Raids," *Los Angeles Times*, August 15, 1996.

[33]Vanora Bennett, "Guns Fall Silent in Chechnya as Lebed Makes Second Visit," *Los Angeles Times*, August 16, 1996.

[34]Richard Boudreaux, "Kremlin Power Struggle Erupts Over Campaign to Defeat Chechens," *Los Angeles Times*, August 17, 1996.

istry's personnel, but rather was "a testimony to the crisis of Russian power."[35]

Lebed's widely publicized insistence that Yeltsin fire Kulikov, punctuated by his "him or me" ultimatum, reflected the would-be peacemaker's nagging frustration over his inability to make the system support his goals from within. It was also a tactical error of the sort that could put him out in the cold should he continue the practice. In so cornering the president, he put Yeltsin in an impossible situation, since whatever Yeltsin's condition of health or day-to-day involvement in politics might have been, he clearly could not submit to overt blackmail by one of his subordinates. Shortly after Lebed threw down the gauntlet, a Chernomyrdin aide responded dryly that "it is the prerogative of the president to evaluate the performance of his ministers."[36] Within hours, Yeltsin declined to accept Kulikov's offer to resign in response to Lebed's charges, instructing the interior minister to remain at his post. Later, both Lebed and Kulikov issued statements of grudging conciliation, indicating their joint awareness that they were fated to work together, for better or for worse.[37]

Later, Yeltsin demonstrably brought Lebed down a peg, instructing him through a spokesman to get on with restoring "a system of law and order" in Grozny, to submit "a report and concrete proposals" for ending the war, and to desist from further grandstanding. Perhaps satisfied at having made his point through his public dustup with Kulikov, Lebed offered Yeltsin an act of contrition in reply, vowing that he would not quit as secretary of the Security Council and

---

[35]Alessandra Stanley, "Two Yeltsin Aides in a Showdown Over Chechnya," *New York Times*, August 17, 1996. It was also a testimony to the almost pathetic inadequacy of Russian military intelligence in the heart of the combat zone. According to one report, the word was out on the streets in Grozny by the beginning of August that a rebel counterattack was imminent and that the civilian populace should hunker down in preparation. Said one Chechen woman, "the fighters said they were coming in on the sixth. They told us to get food and water and go into the basements. They said they were taking the city back." Quoted in Michael Specter, "How Chechens Surprised Foes to Retake Capital," *New York Times*, August 18, 1996.

[36]Ibid.

[37]Alessandra Stanley, "Chechnya Foes Agree to Truce as Yeltsin's Envoy Fails to Oust a General," *New York Times*, August 18, 1996. See also Richard Boudreaux, "Kremlin's Own Chechnya Conflict," *Los Angeles Times*, August 18, 1996.

that he well remembered "who is the country's supreme commander in chief."[38]

As if to add suspicions that the security establishment was out of control, General Pulikovskii next announced that he would resume offensive operations against the Chechen rebels within 48 hours, ordering any residents of Grozny who did not wish to get caught in the crossfire or fall victim to indiscriminate bombing to evacuate the city with dispatch. Only when thousands of frightened civilians began frantically fleeing in all directions to get out of harm's way did the commander of Russian forces in Chechnya, Lieutenant General Vyacheslav Tikhomirov, return from vacation to take over from Pulikovskii. Concurrently, Yeltsin left Moscow on what was said by his aides to be a search for a new vacation resort, amid rampant uncertainty over whether Russian preparations to resume fighting in Grozny had his approval.[39] Left in the wake was a directive putatively signed by Yeltsin assigning Lebed seemingly contradictory instructions on how to deal with the unraveling Chechen situation. In effect, it set Lebed up for a showdown with the on-scene Russian commanders, who more than once had balked at following his wishes. With Chernomyrdin intoning from the sidelines that Lebed "must be given all the support he needs" to bring peace to Grozny, Lebed declared that the Yeltsin "decree" was bogus. He went on to say boldly that there were "solid grounds to doubt that the president of Russia took a direct part in finalizing the text of the orders."[40]

With the lack of direction from Moscow now painfully apparent, and with the returned General Tikhomirov seemingly disposed for the moment to support his errant deputy Pulikovskii in Grozny, the new defense minister Igor Rodionov finally rallied, after a fashion, to Lebed's support. Rodionov declared that General Pulikovskii had been "reprimanded" for issuing an ultimatum to the rebels on his own initiative without higher approval. He did not, however, cancel Pulikovskii's order, thus keeping open the question of who was in

---

[38]Lee Hockstader, "Russia Vows Offensive," *Washington Post*, August 20, 1996.

[39]See David Hoffman, "Russians Prepare to Attack Rebels in Chechen Capital," *Washington Post*, August 21, 1996.

[40]Michael Specter, "Aide to Yeltsin Disputes Orders Over Chechnya," *New York Times*, August 21, 1996.

charge of the military and prompting Sergei Yushenkov—a liberal parliamentarian, former army colonel, and former head of the Duma's Defense and Security Committee—to suggest that "the situation is favorable to a new coup; we are on the brink of a military dictatorship."[41]

Departing on his third trip to Grozny in the midst of this chaos, and apparently now committed to going for broke rather than erring on the side of caution, Lebed adopted a characteristic "lead, follow, or get out of the way" posture and declared: "In the absence of any single commander, my task is to get everybody in hand and tell them all here who is the boss. If they don't like it, they can send in their resignations." He added that he had agreed in principle with Maskhadov on the terms of a cease-fire and that he would ensure that there was no Russian counteroffensive, as had been threatened by Pulikovskii.[42] Lebed added: "There will be no more ultimatums. We will solve this problem by the morning, and we will solve it based on humane considerations and common sense."[43] Asked whether he had authority to impose his will on the balking Russian generals, Lebed replied that "no one has given any one any powers. You simply have to take them, as I am quietly doing." Later that day, he added that he was going to instruct the Russian headquarters in Grozny "to see to it that things will be quiet tomorrow," the day of the threatened counterattack. He also named General Kulikov, remarkably enough, as head of his personal "operational headquarters."[44]

Ultimately, Lebed signed an agreement with Maskhadov that called for a cease-fire and the withdrawal of Russian troops from Grozny, with the prospect that eventually the rebels would surrender their weapons and Russian forces would depart the region entirely. Quite likely, Lebed was helped in inducing the army to withdraw its threat

---

[41]Vanora Bennett, "Russia's Lebed Seeks to Avert Blitz on Chechens," *Los Angeles Times,* August 22, 1996.

[42]Steve Liesman, "Yeltsin Expected Back in Moscow as Cabinet Divides Over Chechnya," *Wall Street Journal,* August 22, 1996.

[43]Michael Specter, "Kremlin Jousts With the Army Over Chechnya," *New York Times,* August 22, 1996.

[44]Lee Hockstader and David Hoffman, "Lebed Moves to Block Russian Attack," *Washington Post,* August 22, 1996.

to launch a counterattack against the rebels within 48 hours by the fact that the just-returned commander of Russian forces, General Tikhomirov, had been Lebed's deputy in the 14th Army in Moldova three years earlier. Back in Moscow, however, Yeltsin went out of his way this time to rain on Lebed's parade, adamantly refusing to meet with his security adviser. Noting that Lebed had "kept promising the voters that he would stop the war in Chechnya if only he had the power," the president complained: "Okay, now he has the power, but unfortunately no results of his work in Chechnya are visible yet."[45] He added sourly: "I am not fully satisfied with Lebed or his work in Chechnya."[46] Clearly Yeltsin was continuing his Byzantine, divide-and-rule approach to Kremlin politics by slapping Lebed down hard, just as the latter's exertions seemed to be producing an interim result that would add further luster to his already impressive image as a doer who could at least remain true to his word.

Perhaps the clearest read on what accounted for all this internecine tugging and hauling was the observation by the London *Economist* that Yeltsin was genuinely ill and that in the ensuing power shuffle, Lebed had "found himself reduced to a last-minute shouting match with his own generals because he had misjudged his priorities as a peacemaker. He had been reaching out to the Chechens but neglecting the sensibilities on his own side."[47] Nevertheless, Lebed succeeded, in the end, in facing down those Russian commanders who had seemed bent on punishing the Chechen rebels with a counterattack. En route home from his third trip to Grozny in less than three weeks, he pronounced confidently: "The military is going to implement my decision. I'm not going to persuade anybody. I have legitimate authority to fulfill the duties I have been charged with. I issue commands. If they don't agree, I will fire them, right up to the deputy minister." Chernomyrdin congratulated Lebed on achieving the cease-fire, but hastened to add that the time had come for other "ministries and agencies and public organizations" to get involved in

---

[45]Quoted in Steve Liesman, "Yeltsin Appears in TV Interview, Criticizes General Over Chechnya," *Wall Street Journal*, August 23, 1996.

[46]Quoted in Michael Specter, "Top Yeltsin Aide and Chechen Foes Sign a Peace Pact," *New York Times*, August 23, 1996.

[47]"Chechnya and Russia: Chaos in Both," *The Economist* (London), August 24, 1996, p. 39.

the development of a longer-term settlement—in effect admonishing Lebed to step back from center stage and to share the spotlight with the rest of the bureaucracy. Yeltsin, too, phoned Lebed with a hedged note of congratulations, praising his cease-fire accomplishment as a "first step," while maintaining an arm's length from his security adviser by adding that any permanent settlement would have to retain Chechnya as "an inseparable part of the Russian Federation."[48]

It remains to be seen how much of this will hold and what it implies for the Lebed-Yeltsin relationship, let alone for Lebed's prospects as an effective Kremlin insider in the now-shaky Yeltsin administration. The best that can be said is that Lebed has managed a remarkable short-term achievement, though at the cost of drawing battle lines with the rest of the Moscow political establishment and further polarizing public opinion: communist and hard-line nationalist elements now openly grouse about a "sellout" of Russian interests to the Chechens. Following his successful conclusion of a tentative cease-fire agreement with Maskhadov, Lebed lamented that he could hardly hope to honor his promise to bring peace to the region when so many people around the president "want to torpedo the process." Queried as to how long he thought it might take to arrive at a final and durable settlement, an exhausted Lebed simply shrugged his shoulders and replied: "Ask me something easier."[49]

No doubt one powerful reason for all the rear-guard efforts to sabotage Lebed's shuttle diplomacy was a jealous resentment among many in Moscow of the former general's ability to succeed where others had failed—or failed to try—plus an awareness that any success on his part at being the architect of an end to the war would advance him appreciably toward his goal of succeeding Yeltsin as Russia's president. No other Russian leader of like seniority could have pulled off such dramatic predawn forays into enemy territory to deal on equal terms with rebel commanders as did Lebed, wholly on the strength of his personal magnetism and his credibility and rectitude as a former military professional.

---

[48]Alessandra Stanley, "The Guns Fall Silent in Chechnya's Capital," *New York Times*, August 24, 1996.

[49]Ibid.

Lebed's willingness to go to the mat and stage a public showdown with Yeltsin more than once over the resolution of the war in Chechnya may well have reflected a calculated gamble on his part that however much his enemies in the president's inner circle might conspire to undermine him, he could count on the support of the Russian people, most of whom are sick of the war.[50] The fact that Yeltsin has not yet moved to unburden himself of his troublesome security adviser after having been safely returned to office with the latter's assistance undoubtedly attests to his reluctance to alienate the constituency that accounts for Lebed's political strength. For his own part, Lebed has made no effort to hide the fact that he himself draws great confidence from the support of that constituency: "They [Yeltsin's deputies] think that they have lassoed me and that I have to obey and play by the rules. But I am not a clerk. Eleven million people are behind me."[51]

SURVIVING IN KREMLIN POLITICS

The events of August 1996 prompted by the resumption of fighting in Chechnya added up to a political test of the first order for Lebed. Yet the new security chief was anything but unprepared for those challenges, since he had received his initial baptism of fire in Kremlin intrigue even before the dust of the July 3 runoff election had settled. Indeed, he prompted a clash with Chernomyrdin the very first day of the latter's reappointment as prime minister by Yeltsin, when Chernomyrdin all but drew a line in the sand in reply to Lebed's bold reach for a broadened Security Council charter: "I am not going to give away anything to anyone," said Chernomyrdin archly. "I don't do anything that is not in my province. Nor am I going to give away anything to anyone or shift any of my powers to anyone." Then, seemingly reaching out for a piece of Lebed's turf, he added: "As to everything pertaining to security and law and order, there will be enough work for everyone."[52]

---

[50]On such a possibility, see in "In Chechnya, Anything Is Possible," *The Economist* (London), August 17, 1996, p. 40.

[51]Quoted in Stanley, *New York Times*, August 17, 1996.

[52]Quoted in Alessandra Stanley, "Yeltsin Appeals to Nation to End Political Breach," *New York Times*, July 5, 1996.

Lebed has prompted sparks from Chubais as well, and he may even encounter a brick wall in Yeltsin himself should his probes into high-level government corruption reach too close to home.[53] In all events, he will almost certainly experience a decline in popularity in due course as his novelty wears off and he settles in as a familiar fixture of the Kremlin establishment. Once that occurs, he will become yet another Kremlin lightning rod to share in absorbing blame for the Yeltsin government's failings. On this point, an analyst from the All-Russian Center for the Study of Public Opinion (VTsIOM) cited a "rapid rise in all sorts of positive expectations regarding [Lebed's] promise as a national leader, imparting to him a host of virtues and giving him the halo of a legendary warrior, if not a savior of the Fatherland, who has come to bring in order."[54] Should Lebed fail to live up to these hopes, said this commentator, it could prompt a severe backlash among his constituents.

Relatedly, another commentator observed: "So far, Lebed has been the only bold figure in the public eye and the only hope for change. . . . If Lebed is sincere in his desire to end the war in Chechnya, he must start a 'war' in Moscow. To win it, the general might need powers so extensive that the whole thing might look like a transition of power. If this does not happen, Lebed, sooner or later, will be blamed for a failed settlement process and share General Rutskoi's fate."[55]

Along the way, Lebed will need to be on guard for multiple snakes in the grass. Korzhakov, to mention but one, is said to have feared Lebed's coming and evidently suspects, despite Lebed's denials, that the former general had a hand in engineering his ouster. He has not yet vacated his Kremlin office and could yet find occasion to retaliate

---

[53]Lebed has openly declared that corruption has reached "right up to the government level." Interview on Russian Public Television First Channel Network, Moscow, July 1, 1996.

[54]Lev Gudkov, "The Kingmaker," *Segodnya*, June 29, 1996.

[55]Roman Stoianov, "Lebed Is the Only Hope," *Nezavisimaia gazeta*, June 25, 1995.

in kind.[56] Indeed, some have suggested that Korzhakov's mini-coup attempt was an early test of strength toward that end that failed.[57]

Chubais also may have had a change of heart after watching Lebed in action. Although he initially had only good words to say about his new Kremlin colleague, Yeltsin's staff chief was finally driven to deal Lebed a mild comeuppance for appearing to be too hungry and in too much of a hurry. "This demand of Aleksandr Ivanovich Lebed for broader powers," he said reproachfully, "is a serious mistake for a novice state leader." Chiding Lebed for his heavy-handed remarks on religion in particular, Chubais added delicately, yet unambiguously, that there were "some shortcomings regarding the balance and profundity of his statements."[58]

For all his detractors and potential enemies, however, Lebed has allies upon whom he will be able to call for political fire support as needed. For example, former army Lieutenant General Lev Rokhlin, a top Russian commander during the early phase of the war in Chechnya and now head of the Duma's Committee on Defense and Security, could be an especially helpful comrade-in-arms in a pinch. Two days after Yeltsin's reelection, Rokhlin said of Lebed that "he has qualities which will help him do his work. He has ambition. . . . He has will power. He certainly is no fool. . . . It's not in his nature to fawn over people. He faces a simple choice: Either he will fade into obscurity or he will achieve something."[59] Significantly, Rokhlin quickly endorsed Lebed's announced candidate for defense minister, Colonel General Igor Rodionov.[60]

Indeed, Yeltsin's announcement on July 17 that General Rodionov would replace Grachev as defense minister constituted an important bureaucratic victory for Lebed and did much to restore his credibility

---

[56]See David Hoffman, "Yeltsin Dismisses Three Hard-Line Aides from Key Positions," *Washington Post*, June 21, 1996.

[57]See "Putsch and Shove," *The Economist* (London), June 22, 1996, p. 47.

[58]Quoted in Michael R. Gordon, "Russian Vote Sets off Battle, This Time in Yeltsin's Camp," *New York Times*, July 6, 1996.

[59]Interview by Yevgeny Kiselev on the "Hero of the Day" program, Moscow NTV, July 5, 1996.

[60]Michael R. Gordon, "Key Russian Legislator Accuses Leading Military Officers of Graft," *New York Times*, July 10, 1996.

as a central player on the new Yeltsin team—after several days in which he had lost points in intramural sparring with Chernomyrdin and Chubais. Earlier, Lebed's seemingly hasty advocacy of Rodionov within days of his own appointment as security adviser, and more importantly his peremptory announcement (incorrect, as it turned out) that Yeltsin would name a successor to Grachev on June 24 or 25, had painted him neatly into a corner and had set him up for a substantial loss of face, to say nothing of political clout, had someone other than Rodionov ultimately been given the nod by Yeltsin. The longer it took for Grachev's successor to be named, the more it appeared that Lebed was standing on thin ice.

Yeltsin's ultimate willingness to accept Lebed's counsel on the appointment of Rodionov to replace Grachev was a resounding testament to Lebed's access and influence, at least in the defense and security sphere. It continued a long tradition of selecting defense chiefs from the uniformed ranks, despite vocal calls from reform circles that the defense minister should be a civilian. It also showed the president's willingness to grant such an important post to an independent who was not a Yeltsin acolyte. Rodionov was known not to be enamored of Yeltsin personally and to have campaigned aggressively for Lebed before the June 16 election.[61] Accordingly, he can be expected to be a strong Lebed spokesman in the defense ministry. Rodionov's appointment completed the shake-up in the Yeltsin administration's defense and security sector that had begun in the immediate aftermath of the election with the dismissal of Grachev and the so-called "party of war."

For his part, Rodionov's remarks were balanced and pragmatic. He commented, for example, that "too much effort and too many resources have been invested in the arms race." He admitted further that "not a single regiment in the Russian army could be prepared for combat within two to three hours." As for East-West security relations and the thorny issue of NATO enlargement, he said that he supports "more extensive contacts with NATO, to promote the partnership, mutual trust, and the exchange of experiences and detente, and that he could not endorse "a policy that seeks to satisfy our own

---

[61]See Carol J. Williams, "Yeltsin Taps Nationalist as Defense Minister," *Los Angeles Times,* July 18, 1996.

megalomania, claiming that no problem in Europe or in any other region of the world can be solved without Russian participation in it." He even said that he sees no "direct external threat to Russia" and that "the greatest threat comes from within."[62]

How effective Rodionov will be as a military reformer is another matter. He embarks on his new assignment carrying baggage from a darker past, when he was the senior on-scene commander who ordered Soviet troops to attack peaceful protesters in Tbilisi, Georgia, in April 1989, in a confrontation that left nineteen civilians dead and earned Rodionov the epithet "butcher of Tbilisi." Commander of the Transcaucasian Military District and military commandant of Tbilisi at the time, Rodionov has since staunchly defended his role in that nasty episode, insisting that he was simply following orders from Gorbachev's Kremlin.[63] Rodionov's supporters maintain that he took the fall for a decision made by the Soviet Politburo. Having been rusticated ever since to the relative backwater of the General Staff Academy, he has been rehabilitated in the minds of many supporters because of his unshaken reputation for moral probity and incorruptibility.[64] Most of Russia's current military elite got to know him during their earlier passage through the General Staff Academy as students.

Rodionov's effectiveness as defense minister will be further helped by the high regard in which he is held not only within the uniformed ranks but also across the political spectrum. True enough, some defense experts in Moscow, notably the deputy head of the Duma's Defense and Security Committee Aleksei Arbatov, have maintained that better choices could have been made from the perspective of modern-day professional competence and management ability. Yet the appointment makes sense when one considers the balancing game Yeltsin seems to be playing in surrounding himself with subordinates who will be responsive to him rather than inclined to build power centers of their own. Rodionov offers a conservative counter-

---

[62]Quoted in David Hoffman, "Lebed Choice Gets Defense Post," *Washington Post*, July 18, 1996.

[63]See Michael R. Gordon, "Choice of Defense Minister Proves a Victory for Lebed," *New York Times*, July 18, 1996.

[64]Neela Banerjee, "Yeltsin Appoints an Ally of Lebed to Defense Post," *Wall Street Journal*, July 18, 1996.

weight to the more liberal Chubais at the senior working level, and both serve to balance the prospects of Lebed and Chernomyrdin as would-be successors to Yeltsin.[65] Unlike Grachev, Rodionov enjoys widespread popularity among the troops and is committed to military reform, having openly backed the eventual development of a smaller and better-trained professional military that is less conscript-heavy than the current Russian army.

The question of questions is whether Lebed, in the end, will be able to coexist with Yeltsin. The former general who was once the Russian president's harshest critic has since declared that he is now standing "shoulder to shoulder" with Yeltsin.[66] He insists that he has coordinated his policy agenda closely with Yeltsin, that many provisions in his campaign program coincide with the president's, and that he now has the "potential authority" to implement them.[67] Nevertheless, he may well prove uncontrollable by his senior sponsor.

For his part, Yeltsin may soon come to regard Lebed not as an asset but as a rival to be contained. As the former reformist legislator, Anatoly Shabad, recently pointed out, "two bears can't live in the same den."[68] Echoing that assessment, the able Moscow political commentator Tatyana Malkina noted that Lebed "does not show any traces of obedience," as reflected in his comment that he did not intend to "bother himself" with any introspective thoughts as to how well he fits in with other Kremlin officials. Beyond that, said Malkina before the July 3 runoff, there is the more basic question of "how two men with very similar characteristics—one of whom is almost officially president-2000, whereas the other is not yet president-1996—

---

[65]Arbatov suggested that it would be better if such appointments were made "proceeding from the criterion of professionalism," but added that "these are internal, very sly compromises relating to the balance of power within the executive branch." He further commented that Yeltsin, by such appointments, was seeking to regulate the authority parcelled out to his top deputies. Quoted in Williams, *Los Angeles Times,* July 17, 1996.

[66]Interfax, Moscow, June 22, 1996.

[67]Aleksandr Lebed, "I Know What I Am Doing, I Know How to Do It. The Election Is Over for Me, I Did Not Become President, But I Made My Choice," *Trud,* June 28, 1996.

[68]Quoted in Lee Hockstader, "Lebed's Meteoric Ascent," *Washington Post,* June 25, 1996.

can coexist in the Kremlin."[69] Similarly, the London *Economist* commented that Yeltsin would be ill-advised to grant Lebed excessive authority or place too much faith in him, since one of the few things indisputable about the former general is his "vaulting ambition."[70] At bottom, Yeltsin probably regards Chernomyrdin more than Lebed as his preferred successor, if only because of his largely shared political values with Chernomyrdin and Lebed's all-too-impertinent comments about Yeltsin since the election.

It might well be good for Yeltsin, for Lebed, for Russia, and for East-West relations in equal measure, once the mess in Chechnya subsides, if the Russian president could effectively instruct his new security adviser to desist from further grandstanding and buckle down to useful work that plays to his greatest strengths, notably in reforming the military and fighting crime. Indeed, there is a strong likelihood that Yeltsin may already have made the first steps toward trying to do exactly that. In late July, he signed a decree establishing a new Defense Council presided over by him personally and including as members Prime Minister Chernomyrdin, Defense Minister Rodionov, Foreign Minister Primakov, and Lebed, among numerous others. The announced secretary of this new high-level deliberative body was not Lebed, but Yury Baturin, Yeltsin's Security Council chief for the preceding three years and an acknowledged liberal.[71] Although it remains to be seen whether this new entity will have anything like the responsibilities and clout of the former Soviet Defense Council under Brezhnev and his successors, it clearly has cast Lebed not as primus inter pares, but only as one among several equals in the defense and security sector. According to one report, the new organization will have a staff substantially larger than Lebed's Security Council, with a total of 53 members.[72]

---

[69]Tatyana Malkina, "Aleksandr Lebed Has Assumed His Duties as Savior of the Fatherland," *Segodnya*, June 19, 1996.

[70]"General Uncertainty," *The Economist* (London), June 29, 1996, p. 18.

[71]Timothy Heritage, "Yeltsin Creates Council to Advise on Defense," Reuters dispatch, July 25, 1996.

[72]Vitaly Marsov, "Boris Yeltsin Has Created A Defense Council and Appointed Yury Baturin As Its Head," *Nezavisimaia gazeta*, July 26, 1996. See also Martin Sieff, "Yeltsin Impairs Lebed With Defense Panel," *Washington Times*, July 26, 1996.

In sum, after a splashy entry into Kremlin politics between mid-June and early July, Lebed has today pretty much dropped off the front pages and out of public visibility, apart from his recent high-profile role in trying to end the newly resurgent war in Chechnya. This is perhaps as it should be if he is to leave his mark as Yeltsin's right-hand man on security matters. Further, it need not necessarily be a bad omen for Lebed's longer-range ambitions. In such a low-profile-insider posture, he has the option of being an obedient public servant and thereby retaining the high ground, which would allow him to resign on principle at any time should his sense of honor become compromised by the realities of survival in the Kremlin pressure cooker. That could put Lebed in a win-win posture for the longer run.

For the moment, however, no one can say what Lebed would be like as Yeltsin's successor. Indeed, the question itself is premature. Yeltsin's campaign strategist Vyacheslav Nikonov has portrayed Lebed as "an empty glass" whose ultimate content remains to be determined. He adds that Yeltsin made a "masterful" move in creating three power bases within his administration, with Chubais as the balancer between Chernomyrdin and Lebed, the latter of whom now occupies the inside track.[73]

Yet Lebed is by no means a shoo-in to replace Yeltsin. He is currently locked in a high-stakes struggle with Prime Minister Chernomyrdin for preeminence in Yeltsin's shadow, and Chernomyrdin will be as strong a contender as Lebed as long as Yeltsin remains healthy enough to complete his second term. Should Yeltsin fail before that time, of course, Lebed may be able to ride the wave of his still-widespread popularity and retain the lead. Alternatively, his pushful and sometimes abrasive style may soon wear thin on other Kremlin officials with whom he must deal. He could easily self-destruct rather than grow into his new assignment.

Yet with Grachev and the "party of war" gone, the future seems to be Lebed's to lose. Chastened by domestic and foreign criticism of his baser remarks since the election, he freely confesses that he is "now somewhat shy of using the wrong word." He further insists that he is

---

[73]Quoted in Carol J. Williams, "Yeltsin Strategist Turns Sights on Buoying Support for Reformers," *Los Angeles Times*, July 27, 1996.

genuinely committed to not turning the clock back, thus underscoring that "we are not going to botch things again, not a second time."[74]

Moreover, Lebed has no objective need to wage offensive war against Chubais and Chernomyrdin, however threatened they may feel by him. His main nemesis was Grachev, and Grachev is now out of the picture. Korzhakov was, in effect, a moat protecting Yeltsin as the president's appointments secretary, bodyguard, and ultimate confidant. With Korzhakov, Soskovets, and Barsukov today out of the picture, Yeltsin "now has no one left that he can call close to him," in the incisive view of Moscow political analyst Lilia Shevstsova.[75] Instead, he is playing a divide-and-rule game. With the "party of war" thus broken up and dispersed, Lebed can now claim the best of two worlds. He was not directly involved in their ouster, yet he undoubtedly benefited from it, in that yet another source of competition in intrigue was eliminated—or at least cut down to manageable proportions. (Korzhakov remains Yeltsin's friend, and thus is far from removed from the picture for good.)

Yeltsin's near-simultaneous dismissal of Grachev and the "party of war" trio of Korzhakov, Soskovets, and Barsukov, and his delicate balancing act among Lebed, Chernomyrdin, and Chubais, have been politically inspired moves, even though too focused on personalities to contribute much toward institutionalizing an enduring system of checks and balances within the executive branch. His elimination of the position of vice president, after Rutskoi tried to exploit it to bring down the presidency in 1993, left him without a ready mechanism for orderly leadership transition. By provision of the 1993 constitution, should Yeltsin die in office or become incapacitated, Chernomyrdin, as prime minister, would become acting president for three months until new elections could be held. That would open an arena for intense jockeying to the finish along with Chernomyrdin, Lebed, and Zyuganov, among possible other contenders yet to emerge.[76]

---

[74]Radio Mayak Network, Moscow, June 27, 1996.

[75]Quoted in Michael Specter, "A Shrewd Act of Self-Preservation," *New York Times*, June 21, 1996.

[76]With respect to Lebed's likely fortunes in such a showdown, one American editorial forum not normally given to such opinion ventured that there were worse alternatives to contemplate than "the ascension of a tough transitional figure along the lines of

For his part, Lebed now controls Russia's defense and security policy portfolio and commands access to the president, at least in principle, on those issues that legitimately concern him. What will mainly obstruct his hopes to rule Russia in the future are the independent ambitions of Chubais and Chernomyrdin. Chernomyrdin, in particular, has thrown his hat into the ring for the next election in 2000 by declaring that he has "not ruled out" running for president.[77]

As for Lebed's near-term prospects, much will depend on the outcome of the continuing drift in Moscow over the fate of the latest cease-fire in Chechnya and the controversial security adviser's role in bringing that watershed development about. As this report goes to press, Lebed has negotiated a framework agreement with the Chechen resistance that, for the first time in 20 months of war, has produced a genuinely promising end to the conflict and has postponed a final ruling on the status of the contested Russian republic until December 31, 2001. That, in turn, has allowed Lebed to declare the war "over." It also has elicited grudging acknowledgment by Chernomyrdin that the plan was "coordinated" with Yeltsin.[78]

Predictably, however, Lebed's achievement has also prompted a studied distancing act by Yeltsin's principal deputies, feeding well-founded suspicions in both Moscow and the West that the would-be leader of Russia is being set up by his detractors for a massive fall.[79] Chernomyrdin, for example, took pains to point out that Lebed's plan "needed a lot of extra work." Yeltsin's chief of staff Anatoly Chubais similarly noted that he was "far from euphoric that all the problems have been solved."[80] For own his part, President Yeltsin has remained conspicuously mute on the matter.

Kemal Ataturk, whose secular nationalism helped lay the foundation for Turkish democracy." "Get Well Soon," *Wall Street Journal*, July 18, 1996.

[77]ITAR-TASS, Moscow, July 4, 1996.

[78]Vanora Bennett, "'The War Is Over,' Lebed Says as Chechen Accord Signed," *Los Angeles Times*, August 31, 1996.

[79]See, for example, Alex Alexiev, "Can Lebed Ride His Apparent Success in Chechnya to Ever Greater Glory?" *Los Angeles Times*, September 1, 1996.

[80]Richard Boudreaux, "Kremlin Waffles on Chechen Peace Pact," *Los Angeles Times*, September 3, 1996.

Lebed is all too aware that some long knives are out for him. During a Moscow television call-in show in which he sought to take his case directly to the people in prime time, he was asked by the moderator for his reaction to a recent newspaper remark that Kremlin forces were plotting to undermine his peace plan in order to block his ambitions to succeed Yeltsin as president. Answered Lebed forthrightly: "There's something to it, really."[81] More boldly yet, he telegraphed several days earlier his complete lack of intimidation by Chernomyrdin and Chubais when he declared that "it's become a fact today that the best politicians are in the military."[82] Perhaps significantly, Lebed has elicited the support of defense minister Rodionov for his negotiated plan to end the war.[83] It will be interesting to see how that declared support plays itself out.

All of this would appear to have placed President Yeltsin rather over a barrel, in that it has positioned Lebed on the high ground either way, with the equally serviceable options of resigning on principle should Yeltsin fail to support the peace process, or else charging betrayal by the Yeltsinite "pseudo-reformers" should he be sent packing for having exceeded his charter. One thing that could undo all of this, of course—quickly and perhaps disastrously—would be for rebel forces to renege on their declared commitment to peace with a semblance of honor for Russia and to resume fighting for total stakes, thus allowing Yeltsin to make a scapegoat of Lebed and jettison him for cause for having been snookered by the enemy. There is much behind the observation of one American reporter that by his aggressively proactive initiatives in Chechnya since the rebel counterattack on August 6, Lebed has "irrevocably hitched his political future to the fate of peace in the separatist southern republic."[84] Yet however this saga ultimately works itself out, it

---

[81]Ibid.

[82]Alessandra Stanley, "Lebed Says Chechen Rebels Agree to Press Peace Talks," *New York Times*, August 31, 1996.

[83]Michael Gordon, "Chechen Peace Pact Draws Fire in Kremlin," *New York Times*, September 3, 1996.

[84]Carol J. Williams, "Lebed Ties Political Fate to Chechen Peace Pact," *Los Angeles Times*, September 1, 1996.

would seem a safe bet that it is not likely, in and of itself, to end Lebed's political career over the longer haul.[85]

In all events, in establishing and nurturing this hotbed of intrigue and caprice directly below him that has pitted factions against factions, with the leaders of each equally suspicious of one another yet dependent on Yeltsin, the Russian president has built a jury-rigged system of executive-branch governance that, in the astute words of another American reporter, "has stretched the meaning of creative tension."[86] Sergei Karaganov, a well-placed and perceptive Yeltsinite insider, foresees an eventual end to such intrigue and a long period of Kremlin stability once the immediate post-election elbowing for position is over. He further anticipates a "considerably more stable" situation in the country than that which exists today.[87] Yet however likely such a development may be in the months ahead, there is little sign in Moscow at present that it has taken significant root. For Western observers of Russian politics, that means that Kremlinology has earned a new lease on life, at least for the near term. For all the continued hopes in the West for untrammeled Russian democratization and reform, the Moscow political scene today has much in common with that of Machiavelli's Florentine Italy.

---

[85]One Western expert has cleverly suggested that even in the worst case of a peace settlement undone by rebel perfidy, Lebed could turn the tables by peremptorily insisting that Chechnya be expelled from the Russian Federation and forced to sink or swim on its own. See William E. Odom, "Chechnya, Freedom and the Voice of Yeltsin's Past," *Washington Post*, August 28, 1996.

[86]Michael Specter, "Yeltsin's New Kremlin," *New York Times*, July 18, 1996.

[87]Cited in "Yeltsin's Election Will End Power Struggles in the Kremlin," *Suddeutsche Zeitung* (Munich), July 3, 1996. See also Karaganov's interview with Dmitri Orlov, "A Lightning Prognosis," *Rossiiskiye vesti*, July 5, 1996.

Chapter Ten

IMPLICATIONS FOR THE WEST

From an American perspective, Lebed's recent rise to power is, as Mark Twain said of Wagnerian opera, not so bad as it sounds—at least so far. To say the least, it is an oversimplification to suggest that Lebed has "disdain for current U.S. policies" and that his appointment "considerably strengthens Kremlin forces termed 'hard-liners' in the West."[1] Actually, quite the contrary may be the case. Despite some early sharp flashes over the NATO expansion issue, and setting aside his frank distaste for what he considers to be debased American values, Lebed has shown little ingrained animus toward the West that would predispose him toward confrontation. Asked after the election for his attitude toward the West, Lebed replied: "I have no attitude. We are friends with everybody. We are trading with everybody. We do not want to fight anybody. We have no territorial claims against anybody. Nor will we accept them from anybody."[2] A few days later, he said with regard to the West that "I see no particular problems. . . . you scored a victory in the cold war, so good for you, my congratulations." As for Moscow's economic and security relations with the leading countries of the West, he added: "There is always room for improvement. We have just begun our cooperation. The future is looking good."[3] If he can be taken at his word, this message strikes a tone that Western policymakers should regard as encouraging. Depending on how they approach Lebed,

---

[1]Katrina Vanden Heuvel and Stephen F. Cohen, "Russia's Judgment Day?" *The Nation*, July 8, 1996.

[2]Interview on Russian Public Television First Channel Network, Moscow, July 1, 1996.

[3]Moscow Mayak Radio Network, July 6, 1996.

they may find in him either an antagonist or a businesslike, if sometimes difficult, workmate in security affairs.

So far, the Clinton administration's posture of guarded optimism regarding the implications of Lebed's rise has been the right one. Two especially important first steps were the recent separate meetings held in Moscow with Lebed by U.S. Ambassador Thomas Pickering and Vice President Al Gore. The State Department's chief spokesman, Nicholas Burns, praised Yeltsin's broadening of his base by enlisting Lebed. Another analyst at State added that "the important thing is that Lebed is singing Yeltsin's song."[4] NATO's leaders too have voiced their approval of Lebed in principle. According to NATO's senior adviser for Eurasian affairs Christopher Donnelly, Secretary General Javier Solana has stated that it is dangerous for Russia's military to be riven by internal weakness and that Lebed's determination to make the Russian military strong and controllable is applauded and welcomed by NATO.[5]

One lingering concern, to recall a point noted earlier, is that Lebed's pattern of insubordination while he was 14th Army commander in Moldova may not bode well for the enduring interest of the West in promoting civilian control of the military in a democratic Russia. Having often stressed the importance of Russia's nuclear posture as the nation's last line of defense, Lebed could also prove nettlesome with respect to the stalled ratification of START II. He can probably be counted on to take a hard look at the START II Treaty before agreeing to ratify out of existence what he has more than once described as Russia's ace in the hole, namely, its existing strategic nuclear capability.

The most crucial unknown remains how Lebed will ultimately handle the touchy question of Russian minorities living in the former Soviet republics. Other areas where he may prove prickly could include the question of arms sales to pariah states and the possibility that he might support a turn to reactionary policies at home. It was

---

[4]Quoted in Michael Dobbs, "U.S. Welcomes Appointment, Citing Impact on Election," *Washington Post,* June 19, 1996.

[5]"Diplomatic Panorama," Interfax, Moscow, June 21, 1996. Donnelly added that Lebed had been invited to visit NATO Headquarters in early 1996, but that the former general had been forced to decline owing to his busy schedule.

in part for reasons like these that Ambassador Pickering rightly noted that the U.S. government would like to see Lebed's role confined to military and law-and-order issues.[6] (On the latter count, however, Lebed has declared that he will not sell arms to Pakistan, to the governments of Khaddafi or Saddam Hussein "or their likes," or to unstable African governments.[7])

Dimitri Simes was absolutely right—to a point—when he recently argued that the time has come for the United States to "start talking to Russia as a reemerging great power rather than as a psychiatric patient entitled to special understanding and indulgence."[8] Yet it would hardly help for America's leaders to be deliberately confrontational by drawing red lines, before the fact, in its political-military dealings with the new Russian government. As a still-recovering economic and sociopolitical basket case after 74 years of communist misrule, post-Soviet Russia remains a raw nerve—and one with 27,000 nuclear weapons of sometimes uncertain accountability. We in the West need to remain guardedly respectful of that important and oft-forgotten fact.

Even more than Russia's other leaders, Lebed will not take kindly to being spoken down to by the United States. Surprisingly, given his reputation for being such a straight-talking general, he showed a thin skin in reacting to President Clinton's note of disapproval for his recent pronouncements suggesting religious intolerance: "I don't understand at all what the very esteemed President of the United States of America took such offense at. I am categorically against anyone teaching us how we should live in our land. I would like to see what Americans would do if we landed some Old Believers somewhere in Alabama, who would begin to knock them into shape there, to teach them how to live, what they should believe, and what they should bow to. There are spheres upon which it is simply impolite to encroach. Therefore, I don't see any basis for panic. He evidently got

---

[6]Reported in "Clinton Hails Russian Vote as Spurning of 'Tyranny,'" *New York Times*, July 5, 1996.

[7]Interview by Inna Rogatshi, "Aleksandr Lebed's Alternative for Russia: A Moderate Patriot," *Suomen Kuvalehti* (Helsinki), September 8, 1995, pp. 17-20.

[8]Dimitri Simes, "Russia: Still a Bear," *Washington Post*, July 9, 1996.

the wrong report. That happens sometimes."[9] Clearly, silence would have been the wiser option for Lebed to have adopted on this delicate point.

Yet as touchy as he may be when it comes to perceived ad hominem affronts, there is no reason for Washington to fear the worst from Lebed's rise to influence. However grudgingly, he has admitted that Russia has little choice but to engage the West. He has also granted that the West has much to offer toward helping integrate Russia into the world as a normal power. There is no prima facie reason to believe he will oppose continued, and even expanded, military-to-military contacts with the United States and its principal allies. On the contrary, he has said that there is much to be gained by integrating the Russian military into the world security system. American foreign and defense policymakers should test Lebed on this as soon as possible.

All in all, the United States has nothing to lose and perhaps much to gain by reaching out to engage Lebed actively in an effort to build a mature Russian-American security relationship shorn of romantic expectations. For better or for worse, his success story to date reflects the honest voice of the Russian people. We in the West must accordingly respect it as the legitimate outgrowth of the new Russian democratic process, however imperfect it still may be. We also must recognize and accept that it was of a piece with Russia's ongoing struggle to transform itself into a rule-of-law state. If the West is properly solicitous and inclined to engage today's troubled Russian leadership without the patronizing overlay that has hitherto often triggered bad feelings among Russians of all persuasions, Lebed may well be disposed to respond in kind. If we write him off too soon as a man on horseback who threatens all we have hoped for in Russian reform, however, we could contribute to a self-fulfilling prophecy and live to regret it.

---

[9]"Segodnya" newscast, Moscow NTV, June 30, 1996.

A SAMPLER OF LEBEDISMS

- "I'm a cat that likes to walk by itself."[1]

- "Most Russians don't care whether they are ruled by fascists or communists or even Martians as long as they can buy six kinds of sausage in the store and lots of cheap vodka."[2]

- "Clever people learn from others' mistakes. Fools learn from their own."[3]

- "Lions led by donkeys can't win against donkeys led by lions."[4]

- "I spit on popularity ratings. I live and serve as I see fit."[5]

- "People aren't given teeth just to chew with. They need to be shown from time to time. Strength makes the world go around."[6]

- "I'm a fatalist. I believe a person born to be hanged will never drown."[7]

---

[1] *The Economist* (London), August 28, 1993, p. 17.

[2] "General Awaits Call of Destiny," *Financial Times* (London), September 6, 1994.

[3] Interfax, Moscow, December 28, 1994.

[4] Interview by Wierd Duk and Aleksandr Zhilin, *Elsevier* (Amsterdam), March 10–11, 1995, p. 53.

[5] Interview by I. Morzharetto and V. Perushkin, *Argumenty i fakty*, No. 14, April 1995, p. 3.

[6] Ibid.

[7] Ibid.

- "I never consider 'ifs' and 'ands.' If grandma had a beard, she'd be grandpa."[8]

- "A cat driven into a corner becomes a tiger."[9]

- "There are no impossible tasks, no hopeless situations."[10]

- "Think before you speak, and don't say everything you think."[11]

- "Russia is like a dinosaur. A lot of time is needed for change to reach the tail from the head."[12]

- "Every country's population is divided as follows: Five percent are the smartest and best, and five percent are the most unrepentant scoundrels. Between them is a swamp of 90 percent who go where they're told."[13]

- "Those who profit are the ones at the top. They keep the doughnut for themselves and give the hole to the people."[14]

- "I am not without sins. There cannot be an airborne assault general who has no sins."[15]

- "God created people big and small. Colonel Colt invented his revolver to even things out."[16]

- "I don't get my experience in life from books. One often has to learn the hard way."[17]

---

[8]Ibid.

[9]Interview by Vitaly Knyazev, *Sobesednik*, No. 16, April 1995, p. 3.

[10]Ibid.

[11]Ibid.

[12]Interview by Dimitrina Gergova, *Trud* (Sofia), July 26, 1995.

[13]Interview by Inna Rogatshi, *Suomen Kuvalehti* (Helsinki), September 8, 1995, pp. 17–20.

[14]Election speech by Lebed, Mayak Radio Network, Moscow, May 14, 1996.

[15]"Vesti" newscast, Russian Television Network, Moscow, June 18, 1996.

[16]Mayak Radio Network, Moscow, June 24, 1996.

[17]Quoted in "To Establish Order," *Der Spiegel* (Hamburg), June 24, 1996, p. 131.

- "One finds free cheese only in a mousetrap."[18]

- "He who shoots first laughs last."[19]

- "Yes, I have many enemies. Many enemies adorn a man."[20]

---

[18]Carol J. Williams, "Law-and-Order Candidate Finds Himself in Role of Kingmaker," *Los Angeles Times*, June 18, 1996.

[19]Quoted in Alessandra Stanley, "Scourge on Yeltsin," *New York Times*, January 17, 1996.

[20]Interview by Andrzej Rybak, *Die Woche* (Hamburg), December 1, 1995.

DATE DUE

MAR 0 5 1997		
MAR 0 5 1998		
MAR 2 4 1998		